BEYOND UNIONS AND COLLECTIVE BARGAINING

ISSUES IN WORK AND HUMAN RESOURCES

Daniel J.B. Mitchell, Series Editor

BEYOND UNIONS AND COLLECTIVE BARGAINING
Leo Troy

CYBERUNION
Empowering Labor Through Computer Technology
Arthur B. Shostak

WORKING IN THE TWENTY-FIRST CENTURY
Policies for Economic Growth Through Training,
Opportunity, and Education
David L. Levine

INCOME INEQUALITY IN AMERICA
An Analysis of Trends
Paul Ryscavage

HARD LABOR
Poor Women and Work in the Post-Welfare Era
Joel F. Handler and Lucie White

BEYOND UNIONS AND COLLECTIVE BARGAINING

Leo Troy

M.E. Sharpe
Armonk, New York
London, England

Library of Congress Cataloging-in-Publication Data

Troy, Leo.
Beyond unions and collective bargaining / Leo Troy.
p. cm.—(Issues in work and human resources)
Includes bibliographical references and index.
ISBN 0-7656-0469-8 (hardcover : alk. paper)
ISBN 0-7656-0470-1 (pbk. : alk. paper).
1. Collective bargaining. 2. Shop stewards. 3. Trade-unions—Recognition. I. Title.
II. Series.
HD6971.5.T76 2000
331.88—dc21   99-27840
CIP

Printed in the United States of America

The paper used in this publication meets the minimum requirements of
American National Standard for Information Sciences
Permanence of Paper for Printed Library Materials,
ANSI Z 39.48-1984.

BM (c) 10   9   8   7   6   5   4   3   2   1
BM (p) 10   9   8   7   6   5   4   3   2   1

Dedication

This book is dedicated foremost to the memory of Professor Leo Wolman, who foresaw.... I also dedicate the book to members of my family: Alex Troy, my son, Suzannah B. Troy, my daughter, my daughter-in-law, Dale, and my three grandchildren, Ariel Sarah, Abigayle Hannah, and Rachel Ilana.

I wish to memorialize two friends who passed away before this book was completed. My colleague, John P. Cullity, with whom I spent many hours discussing the contents, and Leo Wolman, both of us having been students of his at Columbia University. I also had the great pleasure of serving as Leo Wolman's research assistant at the Old National Bureau of Economic Research.

Finally, I wish to memorialize Julia Kaye, whose early demise deprived all of us who knew her of a warm and abiding friendship.

Contents

Series Editor's Foreword

Unionization rates throughout the developed world are declining, especially in the private sector. While the causes are much debated, the ubiquitous nature of the decline makes it imperative that the phenomenon be studied and its implications explored. The need for study and exploration is especially apparent in the United States, where the union representation rate in the private sector is about one tenth of the workforce.

Basic American labor law developed in the 1930s. At the time, because of the Great Depression, workers dissatisfied with conditions on the job had few options. What economists call the "exit" solution, i.e., quitting, was not attractive since jobs were scarce. Unions were seen by the framers of congressional policy as the viable alternative through which workers could "voice" their dissatisfactions and negotiate solutions.

Obviously, much has changed since the 1930s. During more prosperous times, the exit solution becomes more feasible. In addition, there have been many changes in the workforce in terms of education, occupation, and industry. In addition, management has more options available in terms of human resource policy than the simple Taylorism prevalent in the Great Depression.

Leo Troy, author of this volume, is a distinguished scholar who has long tracked trends in union representation and labor relations more generally. Even those who most fervently believe or hope that changes in top union leadership in the 1990s will reverse the downward trend in unionization would do well to heed Troy's analysis. The Troy volume is a companion to another book in this series on nonunion representation: *Nonunion Employee Representation: History, Contemporary Practice, and Policy* edited by Bruce E. Kaufman and Daphne Gottlieb Taras.

Daniel J.B. Mitchell

Preface

Relations between employers and their employees have been predominantly individual or nonunion in this country ever since the development of free labor markets. However, the character of those relationships has evolved under the impact of changes in how work is done, changes in employment, and the resurgence of competition throughout the world's economies, or what I call the New Age of Adam Smith.

Despite the predominance of nonunion labor relations, public policymakers, specialists, and the public at large have historically focused their attention almost exclusively on the organized relationships between employers and employees. To the extent that any attention was paid to nonunion relationships, they were categorized as personnel relations. Later, this was supplemented with analyses of human resource management in employee-employer relations. But, as this book contends, there is much more going on in the nonunion employee-employer relationships than has thus far been depicted in the literature. I have identified the web of those relationships as the individual system of representation.

Attention to what is going on *Beyond Unions and Collective Bargaining* is timely and of growing importance if only because the organized system in the private economy is in a state of irrevocable decline. I do not envisage the disappearance of the organized system, but I do foresee a future I call the "twilight zone." Today the organized system encompasses little more than 9 percent of all private nonfarm workers, barely above its 7 percent penetration rate at the beginning of the twentieth century and down from its historic peak of 36 percent, reached in 1953.

In view of these facts, I address the origins, development, and characteristics of the individual system of representation. In doing so, my point is to explain what the individual system is and how it works. My viewpoint is not antagonistic to the organized system; instead, it takes account of what has befallen that system and why. It is also my hope, if not my expectation, that this analysis will provide a balanced account of the general subject of employee-employer relations in a market economy.

Finally, one editorial note: the uses of personal pronouns in the text are intended to be neutral in gender.

Acknowledgments

Over the years in which this study was conceived and finally completed, I have accumulated numerous debts. Beginning with the most recent, I owe a great deal to the patience of Daniel J.B. Mitchell, consulting editor, and to the advice and patience of editor Sean Culhane, and to Esther Clark of the editorial staff of M.E. Sharpe. I would also like to thank Irene Glynn for the excellent copyediting job. Librarian Ka Neng Au of Dana Library at Rutgers University, Newark, contributed immeasurably to the references and in general knowledge and advice. Bruce Pearce, librarian at the Industrial Relations Centre, University of Toronto, never stinted in time or effort in responding to inquiries that often went beyond Canadian material. Eugene McElroy, librarian at Rutgers University's Institute of Management and Labor Relations, often provided answers to difficult questions. All three librarians made my work on the references, if not pleasant, certainly tolerable.

From the past, I wish to acknowledge the support of the National Association of Manufacturers (NAM) for enabling me to meet managerial staff and officers at a number of companies, large and small, that were involved in the individual system of representation. We agreed at the outset that while I could quote individuals and documents, they would not be identified. There are not many of them in the work that follows, but I ask the reader to accept the authenticity of these statements.

Certain individuals from the NAM deserve acknowledgment for facilitating interviews with selected companies. In particular, I thank

Arthur Prine, Randy Hale, and Bernard Trimble; all are now retired. The association neither endorsed nor even necessarily agreed with my findings and conclusions.

I thank, too, Edward Potter, president of the Employment Policy Foundation, for his encouragement and reading of an earlier version of the manuscript. He offered many helpful suggestions. I alone am responsible for the content that follows.

Beyond Unions and Collective Bargaining

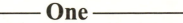

——————— One ———————

A Competitive System of Labor Relations

Purposes, Concepts, and Issues

The individual system of representation, which accounts for more than 90 percent of all employed workers in the private nonfarm labor market, or nearly 90 million men and women at the beginning of the new millennium, is the focus of this study. Despite this predominance in the labor market, it occupies a shadow existence in the literature of labor relations in the United States:

> The organized sector offers IR [industrial relations] researchers increasingly narrow and stagnant areas of exploration. Alternatively, the nonunion sector provides the IR researcher with vast, exciting, and unexplored terrain. More importantly, expanding research into the nonunion sector provides scholars the opportunity to critically evaluate IR as a discipline. (Borgers and Lint 1993)

Likewise, in Britain, the ancestral home of organized representation, it has been observed that "nonunionism and the nonunion firm have been a peculiarly neglected area of research" and that because of the preoccupation of analysts with the organized system, "the subject matter of industrial relations has been defined almost exclusively in terms of the institutions and processes of joint [union-management] regulation" (McLoughlin and Beardwell 1989, p. 1).

Since these observations were made, attention to the nonunion labor market has not changed. To the contrary, despite the revolutionary turnabout in labor relations, the dominance of individual representation and decline of the organized system over the twentieth century (Appendix Figure 1), the "academic interest in unions and bargaining has not waned proportionately . . . [and in fact] academic modeling of union behavior has [even] advanced in recent years" (Lewin, Mitchell, and Zaidi 1997, p. 14). Discussions and analyses of labor markets in academic textbooks must surely lead students to believe that only the organized system exists. To the extent that the nonunion labor market is acknowledged in these expository treatises, it is not viewed as an independent entity but as a fount from which the organized system could find relief from the "American disease" of union decline. Over the past twenty years, labor scholars and unions have repeatedly turned to the nonunion labor market to ask unrepresented workers whether they would join or vote for a union if given the opportunity in a secret ballot election. At no time are workers asked, which do you prefer, individual or organized representation? Variations on that polling theme are surveys whose ostensible goal is to determine the existence of an unfilled gap between the demand for organized representation and its actual extent. The antithetical query, is there an unfilled demand for individual representation? has never been posed. This is ironic in view of the sharp decline of organized representation, which has reduced unions' market penetration to levels last seen on the eve of the Great Depression, even as the nonunion labor market has ascended to near-record levels.

Similarly, ever since the National Labor Relations Board (NLRB) began conducting elections in 1935 to determine whether workers want organized representation or not, ballots against unions are classified as "votes for no union," not votes for individual representation. How, then should votes for no union be construed? In this study, those votes and the survey results opposing organized representation are construed to mean votes for individual representation. The transition from that status to a system occurred in the 1950s. Between the enactment of the National Labor Relations Act in 1935, followed by the policies of the National War Labor Board (NWLB) during World War II, *the content of nonunion labor relations became a tabula rasa* until the 1950s. As employer forms of labor relations established prior to the act of 1935 were wiped out by the

NLRB, employers responded with a variety of ad hoc solutions (Chapter 2). This was followed by policies of the NWLB, which in its administration of wage controls, contributed further to wiping the slate clean of extant nonunion labor relations practices. In fact, armed with powers of compulsory arbitration, the NWLB stimulated the expansion of the organized system even more than the NLRB. The NWLB was formally a tripartite agency, with representatives from unions, the government, and employers. Ostensibly, the employers were surrogates for the nonunion workers, which indicates the inferior status given these workers, even though they constituted the great majority of employees in the labor market. The process of eliminating nonunion labor practices was renewed during the Korean War when another compulsory arbitration body, the Wage Stabilization Board, reiterated the policies of the NWLB. At the end of that war, nonunion labor relations hit their nadir and, conversely, the organized system touched its zenith in the labor market. At that point, the turnabout depicted in Appendix Figure 1 began.

By the early 1950s, as a result of labor law and two regimes of government control over the terms of employment, the pre–New Deal forms of nonunion labor practices were for all practical purposes reduced to nothing or blotted out of existence. A watershed in nonunion labor relations was at hand; a structural change was in the making. At the time, however, because of the mounting successes of the organized system, unions and their adherents came to believe that employers were ready to accept unionization as a fact of life and did not anticipate the new challenge that was just on the horizon. Because economic changes such as the emergence of the new labor market and increased competition occur slowly and imperceptibly, many academic industrial relations specialists analyzing the post–World War II and Korean War years failed to anticipate the beginnings and expansion of the nonunion system. These specialists assumed that collective bargaining and the organized employee relationship were the norms and expected that the future would witness the extension of the union trends of the 1930s and 1940s. At one point, the AFL-CIO was persuaded by academic thinking that a change in employer attitude toward the unionization of their employees had occurred: "By the 1950s and 1960s . . . to a large extent employers did not choose to interfere with their employees' exercise of the right of self-organization . . . [and] if workers chose a union, employers by and large complied with their legal duty to bargain . . . in an honest effort to reach a contract" (AFL-CIO 1985, p. 10).

The misassessment of managerial attitudes toward the unionization of their employees was all the more ironic because management has indeed become even more professional since the 1950s and 1960s, but in the interest of avoiding unionism. The notion that management accepted unionism was based partially on the illusion that collective bargaining could nullify competition in labor costs, epitomized in the phrase that collective bargaining could "take wages out of competition." The policy is not only unattainable but it gives the individual system an advantage in its competition with the organized system. Nevertheless, the AFL-CIO's belief that employers' attitudes toward unionism and bargaining had changed attracted "more academic attention than it won managerial followers" (Harris and Associates 1984, p. 154). Later, after the individual system expanded, academics who may have fostered that view revised their judgment and now concluded that "while executives may have become less emotional in their attitude toward unions, they are not less determined in their opposition to unions than they were 25 years ago" (Steiber and Block 1981, p. 346).

In fact, the possibility of the new system of individual representation was not only unforeseen by both the leaders of organized labor and the academic world but one academic expert believed that the organized system was on the threshold of altering America's society and economy. He predicted that the organized system, which now looked like Goliath, would engender a laboristic society: "Many kinds of employees are organizing themselves into trade unions, and these unions are the most powerful economic organizations of the time. . . . A laboristic society is succeeding a capitalist one" (Slichter 1948, p. 5). Soon after, however, the organized system peaked (1953) and began an uninterrupted decline to the present time.

Concurrently, the experience of the previous twenty years in nonunion labor relations developed into *the contemporary system of individual representation*. The process, a product of Social Darwinism, was stimulated by a dramatic change in the climate of labor relations when the Labor Management Relations Act of 1947 (the Taft-Hartley Act) was enacted; its effects were deferred by the Korean War and the concomitant government regulation of the labor market. The new legislation created an affirmative right of workers not to join a union, absent an agreement requiring membership or the payment of agency fees, and in those states whose laws (right-to-work laws) prohibited such contractual terms. The legal affirmation of a worker's right not to join (as just qualified) gave a new impetus to the embryonic and rudimentary practices that developed into individualism as a system in employer-employee relations (Chapter 2).

During the past two years, a "third way" alternative to the individual and organized systems has been advanced. Some scholars now argue that there is a structure in labor relations that they term Nonunion Employee Representation (NER), which, according to its proponents, represents workers over the terms and conditions of employment and at the same time is not a labor organization within the meaning of the National Labor Relations Act. For more than sixty years, however, the act has addressed this issue and has always found any such form of representation illegal. For that reason, I reject NER as invalid in the United States (Chapter 7).

Because the individual system of representation is an unusual concept in the literature of labor relations, I begin with the question, is it an oxymoron to regard individual representation as a system of labor relations? The word "system" implies regular interaction between distinct elements, which, subject to common forces, construct a cohesive entity. Inasmuch as markets allocate most economic resources, outside of government, through a system produced largely by individual actions through impersonal signals, why should not the same principles apply to individual representation in the labor market? The individual system of representation is, after all, subjoined to the general system of markets. So, yes, conceptually, individual representation in labor relations is a genuine suffix to the general market system, defining, interpreting, and transforming the relationship of individual workers to their employers into a system. Accordingly, the central finding of this inquiry is that there has been a revolution, one that has been virtually unnoticed and unheralded in the industrial relations system of the United States. As just indicated, this transformation began nearly a half-century ago with the switch from an apocryphal dominance of the organized to the actual dominance of the individual system of representation. Since 1953, when the collective bargaining model of labor relations peaked at 36 percent of all private-sector workers (Troy and Sheflin 1985), labor relations in the United States have shifted uninterruptedly to the individual system of representation, and this study contends that the shift is irrevocable.

The study asks next, what makes individual representation a system? How did the system arise? What makes it work? Is the individual model imitative of the organized system, and vice versa? Can it claim any innovations? How extensive is the individual model among major industries and states? Who are the workers who participate in the system? What protects them from employer exploitation and from the competition of the organized system? Alternatively, what protects the organized system from encroachment by the individual system? What is the future of the competitive relationship between the two systems?

Can Individual Representation Be a System?

A collective voice, unionism and collective bargaining, is taken for granted as a system of labor relations. The organized labor movement and most academicians contend that the only meaningful voice that can give expression to employees in the labor market of an open, democratic society is the collective voice. Contrariwise, this study argues that a competitive voice, the individual voice, exists as well. It exists and works because it, too, is an alternative in an open society; it exists and works, too, because the facts in the workplace and, paradoxically, the basic law of labor relations of this country, which was designed to foster the collective voice, the National Labor Relations Act, sustain the individual system of representation.

The conditions requisite for the individual system consist of the several catalysts that have initiated and increased the effectiveness of the individual system of representation. Of paramount importance is the difference in the markets in which the two competing systems function. The individual system is more consonant with competitive markets, both those in which the product is sold and those in which labor is recruited. In contrast, the organized system is more consonant with less competitive markets. Before the enactment of the National Labor Relations Act, the organized system drew its strength from a monopolistic position in the labor market, a market described by economists as lacking many substitutes, where the number of people employed in a given type of occupation was relatively unresponsive to wage increases (i.e., the unemployment effect was small relative to a wage increase). These conditions characterized the skilled workers among whom the first and most successful unions were established (and which gave rise to the term *trade union*). When the National Labor Relations Act was adopted in 1935 and upheld by the Supreme Court in 1937, the law augmented the market's monopoly of the organized system and extended it to workers beyond skilled tradesmen. The combination of monopolistic markets and monopolistic law increased the market distinctions between the organized and the individual systems of representation. Indeed, those differences lie at the heart of the inverse-mirror-image behavior of the two, growth versus decline, which became acutely evident following the end of World War II.

Stimulated by freer international trade, which I call the New Age of Adam Smith, technological changes, and changes in the structure of employment, the two systems responded differently to the same environmental pressures. The concordance of these pressures enhanced the competitive, the comparative advantage, of the individual system, while exposing the vulnerability of the organized system in the years that followed. The consequences of the differential impact were the ascendancy of the individual and the slump of the organized system. Measured by market share, the individual system rose from its nadir of 64 percent of the labor market to its present level of 91 percent. Conversely, the extent of organization of the organized labor market (density) peaked in 1953 at 36 percent and has since plunged to 9 percent of the labor market.

Although these developments opened representation in the labor market to an alternative in labor relations, by themselves the new concepts and practices could not establish the system of individual representation. The fundamental requisite of the individual system of representation is the demand of workers and employers to establish and maintain the system. Employers' preference for a nonunion system can be taken as a given; in fact, as is reported in Chapter 8, unions, and universities, when acting in the capacity of employers, also exhibit the same preference for individual dealings with employees as employers in the private labor market. The demand of workers for individual representation, like the system of individual representation itself, is camouflaged by the various surveys of nonunion workers' attitudes toward joining unions and by the statistical presentations of the NLRB, as noted earlier. Despite their indirectness, the government's statistics reveal that there is a separate and independent demand by nonunion workers for individual representation. Because of that separate and independent presence, there is also a model of the system of individual representation, just as there is for collective representation.

A Model of the System of Individual Representation

Any system of labor relations (Dunlop 1958) encompasses employers and employees, their philosophies and policies, the techniques they use to determine the terms and conditions of employment, public policies, and the state of labor markets and the economy. Dunlop summarized an industrial relations system as "an abstraction" addressing "critical variables" with "propositions" subject to "historical inquiry and statistical testing." As the present study demonstrates, the propositions of the individual system are subject both to historical inquiry and statistical testing.

The system of individual representation, as an adjunct of the market system, does what markets do; it establishes a communications system that binds the participants into a rational structure. The individual system, like the organized system, resolves the fundamental issues of employee-employer relations—wages and all other terms and conditions of employment. The building blocks of the individual system, excepting the union, are much the same as those of the organized system: the worker, the employer, the rules of the workplace (absent those of collective bargaining), the communication systems within the workplace, public policies, the labor market, and the national and international economy. Nevertheless, its philosophical orientation differs significantly from the organized system: As the term implies, the system is committed to individualism. In contrast, the organized system's "philosophical/political outlook . . . may be characterized as collectivist utilitarian" (Machan 1981, p. 113). Despite the fact that most nonunion workers regard unionism as unnecessary—irrelevant in fact —(Harris and Associates 1984, p. 29; Farber and Kreuger 1992, Abstract), they share a number of beliefs with union members— the bread-and-butter issue in particular. These beliefs remain central to the employment relationship, individual or organized. However, the two systems differ on how the bread and butter are to be produced and distributed. Under the individual model, *the market (although imperfect)* distributes income between employers and employees. In contrast, because of its monopoly power (self-generated and publicly endowed), the organized system alters the market's *distribution* of income, redistributing some of it from unorganized workers and formerly employed union members to employed union members. The redistributive effect on employers' income is less certain, although it clearly affects the profitability of the enterprise. In the process, the organized system has adversely affected the ability of unionized employers to compete with comparable competitors. (Hirsch 1991; 1997; Long 1993). The individual model swims with the currents of market forces. In contrast, the organized system, like monopolies of business, is in conflict with the markets. As Charles Lindbloom of Yale (a sympathizer of unions), wrote, "the union [is] an anticompetitive institution [operating] in a competitive environment" (Lindbloom 1949, p. 19).

The variables critical to the model of individual representation are the philosophy of individualism and competitive markets. These explain the behavior of the two principal actors in the system: the workers and the employers. The goals of employers are profit maximization consistent with harmonious labor relations. For the employee, the goals are maximization of income, employment security, and optimal working conditions, consistent with harmony in their relations with their employers. The mutual desire of both parties for harmonious relations does not prevent conflict in the nonunion system; it is not an Alice in Wonderland fantasy world. The employment relationship, whether nonunion or union, is frequently characterized by conflicting as well as cooperative characteristics.

The model of the nonunion system puts the individual worker at the center of the system. This view conflicts with the conventional assessment of nonunion industrial relations that puts the employer at the center and treats the individual employee as a passive participant capable only of Pavlovian responses. Perhaps the best response to the question, which of the two participants, workers or employers, is more important to the individual system? is the reply about a century ago of the great British economist Alfred Marshall to a similar question: which is more important in determining price, demand or supply? He replied that, like the blades of a scissors, both are needed. Likewise, without the demand of both the individual worker and the employer, there is no system of individual representation. Without both, the system degenerates into an administrative model of employee relations, or human resource or personnel management.

The individual and organized systems function differently because they serve a number of different interests. In the individual model only the interests of the employer and the individual workers must be reconciled vis-à-vis the market (customers). In the organized system, a union must look after its organizational interests, reconciling those interests with management and with conflicting interests among its membership—younger versus older, skilled versus unskilled, balancing demands of profit sharing against known wage increases, to list some of the important variances in the interests of the membership, and these also vis-à-vis the market (customers). In the organized sector, the union shares with management the governance of employee relations. This important difference sets apart the two systems; it is what nonunion management characterizes as "third party intervention." Governance in the individual system flows from the market, workplace practices, and labor and employment law.

The individual model of representation, which is consistent with the philosophy of the open society, is also part of a general intellectual shift toward individualism of recent years. In reversing the trend toward collectivism in the labor market in Britain, where it had progressed much further than in this country, Phelps Brown, a highly regarded observer of British society and economy, commented:

> Recently a new view of society has come to prevail. The practices of the welfare state and the planned economy have been cut back or reversed. . . . People are no longer seen as dependent on society and bound by reciprocal obligation to it . . . Individuals are expected to shift for themselves. . . . (Brown 1990, p. 1)

Although it is general, the individual system does not encompass all forms of nonunion employee relations; some fall solely within the domain of personnel relations. Likewise, the organized system neither precludes nor abolishes personnel relations, although its role and authority are modified by the regulations of the bargaining agreement. Personnel administration coexists with both systems; it plays a greater role in the nonunion system, but is not a substitute for the individual system of representation. For that reason, the present study differs from those that treat the individual employee as the passive object of the personnel policies of employers (Foulkes 1980). Indeed, the title of Foulkes's book, *Personnel Policies in Large Nonunion Companies*, reveals that it is about personnel practices wherein employee relations exist as an adventitious or "administered" function of the personnel department.

The size of the workforce also does not identify the individual system as something apart: "While all organizations undoubtedly have some informal practices that would qualify . . . [as an industrial relations system], only those employers of a certain minimum size (say, 300 employees) probably have enough [informal practices] so that, considered together, they would be dignified with the label 'system' " (Garbarino 1984, p. 43). In contrast, the NLRB, which determines the magnitude and character of units appropriate for bargaining in the organized system, has ruled that as few as two persons constitute a unit appropriate for organized representation. Why, then, should an arbitrary and much larger numerical standard of 300 apply to the system of individual representation? It is also clear that many independently owned companies and subsidiaries of large corporations have fewer than 300 employees, but in which employee relations, based on the individual, constitute a system.

A similar interpretation is applicable to Garbarino's "administrative model" of nonunion labor relations. It, too, assumes the individual worker has no demand for individual representation. The administrative model equates nonunionism with industrial autocracy: "This model is unilaterally established by the employer and is interpreted and implemented through the internal hierarchical structure of the organization." The workers are treated as passive partners to "implicit contracts," which "refer to the whole set of expectations about wages and working conditions that are held by employers and employees concerning their future relationship on the job" (Garbarino 1984, p. 43). However, if the "administrative model" recognizes contracts between workers and management, implicit notwithstanding, does not that contract require an active role for individual workers? Even some employers operating under the individual system delude themselves into believing that they are practicing the tenets of the administrative model. Actually, the title of Garbarino's study, "Unionism without Unions: The New Industrial Relations?" indirectly highlights the issue central to this study: individual representation as a system of industrial relations. Finally, the evidence indicates that there is more going on than a manipulated partner to a compelled contract. Surely the nonunion complaint systems are more than "pale shadows of the bargained versions" (Garbarino 1984, p. 44). Certainly the Harris study for the AFL-CIO found this to be so (Harris and Associates 1984).

The system of industrial relations beyond unions and collective bargaining is also distinct from human resource management and for the same reason that it is distinct from the "administrative model"—workers' demand for individual representation. For purposes of this study, I define the functions of human resource management to encompass both personnel administration and employee relations. These functions cover the identification and planning of employment needs, recruitment, training and development, job analysis, appraisals of employee performance, benefits, compensation, safety, working conditions and complaint systems, organized or not. (Delery 1997, pp. 150–153; Stone and Meltz 1993, pp. 6–16). These functions are performed in both systems and help sustain the general relationship of employers with employees, but are not a substitute for it, organized or individual.

Human resource management is a more important element in shaping managerial actions in the contemporary system of individual representation. In organized labor relations it coexists with collective bargaining; in the individual system it is a supplement, but not a substitute. Human resource management plays a different role in each system. In the nonunion setting it is both a line and staff operation. In the unionized setting, the line function of human resource management is curtailed in favor of the bargaining agreement and arbitration. In the nonunion setting, the existence of complaint systems also curtails human resource managements' line function, but much less extensively. Other forces, some legal (the decline of "at-will" employment, for example) and, more notably, the economics of human capital, engender major restraints on human resource management's line functions. In fact, the economics of human capital probably exercises greater influence in the individual than in the organized system because of greater managerial flexibility in training and the assignment of work. In general, the relationship of human resource management to both systems of representation is to provide a supply of services. In the individual system, it does not generate the "demand" for the system; only the workers can do that. Nevertheless, human resource management can influence the workers' preferences one way or the other.

Another reason for distinguishing human resource management from the individual system of labor relations is the origin and development of each. Human resource management appeared after the development of the contemporary nonunion system. Moreover, the initial impetus to human resource responsibilities came not from labor relations, but from attention to human rights and to standards of employment:

> In terms of power and sheer numbers of professionals, HRM [human resource management] received perhaps its biggest boost from human rights legislation of the 1960s. . . . A 1976 article by Herbert Meyer even referred to personnel directors as the "new corporate heroes" because their new function was to ensure that companies were in compliance with the complex set of human rights and employment statutes. (Stone and Meltz 1993, p. 5)

Despite the analytical and factual evidence of a system of individual representation, the theory of its existence will surely be contentious. Because of preconceptions stemming from the history of unions and collective bargaining, critics of the market system and of unorganized employee relations reject individualism in industrial relations as a fantasy. To the conventional wisdom, only collective action can be meaningful philosophically and empirically.

The Response of Nonunion Workers to the Model

The observed behavior of unorganized workers is consistent with market theory underlying the model: the majority believe that the market can satisfy their needs and consequently prefer and vote for individual rather than organized representation. The fact that more than 90 percent of private-sector workers in the United States are outside the organized sector cannot be treated as simply a statistical artifact. It is an empirical demonstration, the "participation rate" of workers in nonunionism; it reflects their attitudes favoring individual bargaining, attitudes that surveys and representation election results have turned up with consistency over time.

The principal reasons nonunion workers reject organized representation in favor of individual representation were detailed by the Harris survey for the AFL-CIO in 1984. That survey was and remains the most comprehensive of all surveys of workers' attitudes toward unions. Topping the Harris list of nonunion workers' preference for individual representation was "no need for a union."

Second was, "unions don't make sense for my job." Another reason given in the Harris survey was that "employees are better off without a union" and "prefer to be independent" (Harris and Associates 1984, Table 22, p. 65). Ideological opposition to unionism was minor among nonunion workers, as was simple disapproval of unions. According to the Harris survey, "there is not a huge outpouring of hatred and vitriol against unions" (Harris and Associates 1984, p. 29). Instead, nonunion workers rejected organized representation for pragmatic reason, findings that match the attitudes of nonunion management, who also oppose unionism for pragmatic, not ideological reasons. Summing up its findings on why nonunion workers prefer individual instead of collective representation, the Harris study concluded: "Simply put, [to nonunion workers] the union route is an irrelevant way to solve their work problems" (Harris and Associates 1984, p. 29). For Harris, to also say "to be irrelevant in many ways is the crowning insult for an honorable institution" (Harris and Associates 1984, p. 30) had to be a bitter pill to swallow.

Despite these facts, the collective bargaining model is typically, but incorrectly, treated in the media and in college and university courses as either the dominant or the only system of representation, as already noted. This general misrepresentation applies also to measures of all major industrial sectors of the labor market. Actually, individual representation dominates employee relations in all the traditional strongholds of unionism of manufacturing, construction, road transportation, communications, and mining, as well as in the historic nonunion service sector. Only in railways and in sea and air transportation has individual representation made limited inroads. In each, the conditions requisite for the development of the individual system, competition in particular, have been thwarted by extensive government involvement in the labor relations of these industries.

Despite these facts, the public has a limited and usually incorrect awareness of the scope of nonunionism. The reason for this misperception is that unions still represent many of the country's leading companies in autos, steel, aluminum, mining, railways, construction, road transportation, and apparel. When these companies and their unions bargain collectively, their agreements, and especially their disagreements, attract media attention. Strife always makes news in the labor field, just as it does in politics and personal matters. Meanwhile, in the system beyond bargaining, events go largely unreported and unnoticed, as is typical of many developments governed directly by the marketplace. Public unawareness of the nonunion system is also the result of the "diffusion effect"—the large number and smaller sizes of nonunion enterprises, and their growth and spread throughout the country. Nonunion employers also contribute to the public's unawareness of the size and importance of the nonunion system. For several reasons, they typically avoid calling attention to themselves. Long under attack by academics and others whose sympathies lie with the bargaining system, some nonunion managements deliberately adopt a low profile. Others shun the public spotlight to avoid the appearance of challenging the organized system. Some believe that media avoidance is also union avoidance.

Who Are the Nonunion Workers?

Who are the nonunion workers? Do their demographic differences affect the competition between the individual and organized systems of labor relations? The literature of industrial relations provides extensive data on the characteristics of unions and members, but correspondingly little on nonunion employees, even though such data are readily at hand. Overall, the profile of the nonunion workforce is more congruent with the contemporary and projected labor markets than the organized workforce—an unsurprising congruence inasmuch as it constitutes most of the workforce. However, contrary to the conventional assumption that nonunion employment is largely, or only, domiciled in the service labor market, in fact it dominates the historic industrial centers of the organized system—manufacturing, construction, mining, and transportation as well. Thus, the nonunion system is distributed throughout the labor market and is therefore better positioned to grow and compete in the highly competitive international economies of today and in the new century than the organized system.

Nonunion employees dominate virtually all demographic characteristics. Most are women, most are younger and have more education, most include part-timers and dominate the occupational and geographic profile in all states. Only minorities may be an exception. But, this is not conclusive. Because the statistical data underlying the demographic profiles include government, the minority representation in the private nonunion labor market is probably understated. In particular it affects the representation of women, minorities, and professionals in the unionized profile.

Currently, women are the majority of nonunion employees, over one-half; two decades ago, they comprised only one-quarter of all nonunion employees. The doubling is a result of the rise of service industries and occupations. Historically, these occupations and industries have not been unionized, and the outlook is for their continued expansion on a nonunion basis into the next century. In contrast, the expansion of union membership among women and minorities is predominantly the result of policies fostering unionism in the public sector. Similarly, trends in the profiles of professional and managerial occupations are explained by unionization in the public labor market. Minority workers constitute a larger proportion of the unionized profiles than of either the nonunion or the total labor market. This has been the product of the shrinkage in white-dominated union membership in the private sector, coupled with union growth in the public sector. The greater propensity of minorities to join unions may also have contributed (Harris and Associates 1984; Medoff 1977).

While men are a minority in the nonunion workforce, they continue to dominate the union population, reflecting the history of organized labor since the modern union movement was established near the end of the nineteenth century. Nonunion workers are much younger than the union population, and, like the gender gap, the age gap is widening. In other words, the organized system is aging, a demographic fact that must be worrisome for its long term prospects. Part-time employees have become increasingly important in the general and the nonunion labor market. On the other hand, full-time employees dominate the organized system of industrial relations. Employers' increased reliance on part-timers doubtless reflects efforts to minimize labor costs, especially those arising from mandatory benefit programs. Many in the population, the young and women especially, often find part-time jobs fit their lifestyles. For these reasons, part-time employment is likely to gain even more importance. Like the age and gender profiles, the nonunion/union disparities among part-time workers are attributable to the growth of service-dominated labor markets. The postindustrial labor market affords more part-time job opportunities to women and the young, groups with high participation rates in the nonunion system.

Employment in all industries is not only predominantly nonunion but it has been growing steadily. Among nonfarm industries, the nonunion rate of employment in four of them is more than 90 percent: FIRE (Finance, Insurance, and Real Estate), Services, and Retail and Wholesale Trade. Manufacturing and construction, the industrial heartland of unionism, are well below 20 percent organized, and well below their historic highs of 1953. Today, the most unionized industries are transportation (rail and air), communication, and public utilities. These remain substantially organized because all continue to be subject to varying degrees of government regulation and consequently are less vulnerable to competitive conditions. Geographically, the two systems are drifting apart, the areas of nonunionism growing and the areas of unionism declining.

Who Protects the Nonunion Worker?

Who protects the interests of the individual worker in the nonunion system? Who "negotiates" for the nonunion worker? Primarily, it is the market. As Milton Friedman wrote: "the most reliable and effective protection for most workers is provided by the existence of many employers" (Friedman 1980, p. 246). Even though labor markets are imperfectly competitive, Friedman observed that "[this] is an imperfect world, so competition does not provide complete protection . . . [but] competition is the best, or, what is the same thing, the least bad protection for the largest number of workers that has yet been found or devised" (Friedman 1980, p. 246). Friedman's comment echoes Churchill's observation about democracy—that it is the worst form of government, except for all the rest! Markets may be the worst system of allocating resources and rewarding people—except for all the others.

Paradoxically, labor law, the National Labor Relations Act, contributes to the existence of the individual system of representation. Of course, the thrust of the act has been to encourage unionism and collective bargaining, but even under its original and most prounion version, the Wagner Act of 1935, the National Labor Relations Act also recognized the right of employees not to choose a labor organization to represent them. The original legislation did not specify or encourage this right. Nevertheless, indirectly it implemented the right to nonunionism. In conducting representation elections, the NLRB necessarily had to provide a place on the ballot for employees to reject organized representation. Thus, although only by default, the original National Labor Relations Act gave formal recognition to the existence and right of individual representation. When the act was amended in 1947 by the Labor Management Relations Act (the Taft-Hartley Act), the amended legislation made the individual model an explicit right, subject to the conditions noted above. Moreover, because many of the right-to-work states are among the fastest growing in employment in the nation, the individual system is taking root in the economically expanding sections of the country. Meantime, employers' right to free speech (within statutory limitations spelled out in the amended act of 1947) reversed a dozen years of previous curtailment by the NLRB. Furthermore, unions now could violate employees' rights to join or not to join labor organizations, contributing in another way to the system of individual representation. For those reasons, this study argues that the enactment of the Taft-Hartley Act provided a legal imprimatur to the contemporary system of individual representation.

Employment law, law governing working conditions as distinct from labor relations law, also provides protection to the individual worker and therefore the individual system. Limitations on employment at-will and the enactment of specific conditions of employment have created a web of rights and benefits that compete and substitute for the collective bargaining agreement. While employment law, like labor law, may contravene market determination of employment conditions (Epstein 1992, p. A11), for workers it is seen as a substitute for unions and collective bargaining. In fact, this substitution effect has been identified as one reason for the decline of private sector (the old) unionism (Neumann and Rissman 1984). If unionized, or potential union members, regard employment law as a substitute for collectively bargained protections, why shouldn't workers under the nonunion, individual system of representation assess the substitution effect as applicable to them as well?

From the conventional viewpoint, only institutions that intervene in the market—government and unions—are capable of protecting the worker. Markets are regarded as unfair to workers and must therefore be combated, not relied upon and utilized to serve the interests of any factor of production, workers especially. Unions and government do indeed contribute to the protection of workers, but so do markets. In the end, it is competitive markets and productivity that generate higher living standards.

Yet another economic force, employers' conservation of their investment in the human capital of their employees, protects workers under the system of individual representation. Most would readily agree that a management that misuses the company's physical capital must be regarded as at least wasteful, if not irrational, and would bring about the dismissal of such management. Would not this also apply to an employer misusing the company's most valuable asset, the capital investment in the employee, the training and the experience that are recognized as critical to the profitability of the enterprise? There is a preconception that nonunion employees would be vulnerable to arbitrary treatment and exploitation by employers offering less than competitive compensation, but even in the absence of unions and government policies, human capital investment and competitive markets would enable unorganized employees to avoid or minimize exploitation. When labor markets are not competitive, when employer domination prevails, exploitation can take place. Indeed, there are irrational employers who exploit their employees when competition is limited, just as there are irrational unions that pursue wage policies that price their members out of the market and send them into unemployment.

Yet another economic factor contributing to the viability of the individual system of representation is the "economy of high wages." Paying above the market level has a long history of success in recruiting, training, and retaining the best workforce. It is "paid for" by the increased productivity, better safety, and attendance records of such employees. Competitively, it is the labor cost per unit of production that determines which are the most efficient and competitive companies, not the level of wages, either in the nonunion or union domain. This is the root of the individual system's ability to compete so successfully with the organized system.

Both the individual and collective bargaining systems of industrial relations are decentralized, but many local bargaining agreements are patterned after national standards and are therefore not as reflective of local labor markets as is the case of the individual system. In the nonunion system, decentralization is the theoretical and empirical essence of its compensation policy, including plants of multiplant employers. Statistically, the decentralization of the nonunion system is prompted by the large number and typically smaller size of enterprises. Among multiplant companies there is an increasing trend for local management to fashion local policies in dealing with their employees in order to reflect local market conditions. Reference, or checking it out with corporate headquarters, remains intact, but the degree of local leeway has increased. While the globalization of the economy has compelled the organized system to abandon pattern bargaining steadily, and to fashion agreements in line with local market conditions, they lag the unorganized sector in this practice. While pattern bargaining has steadily lost its importance in collective bargaining (the Caterpillar strike in 1992, for example), unions still adhere to the principle even as the practice wanes, making their ability to adjust to changing market conditions slower and less complete. And the new trade agreements will sharpen the conflict between past practices and new realities:

> Faced with new and more severe economic constraints, union lead-
> ers and the rank and file have been slow to adjust their expectations,
> strategies, and wage demands. (Hirsch 1997, p. 63)

On the other hand, the nonunion system is attuned to local labor
markets, making it more competitive and flexible in meeting the
challenges of the new trade agreements.

Inadvertently, the unions' wage policy, the policy of "taking wages
out of competition," contributes to the individual system. Although
that policy is unattainable because, as just noted, the fundamental basis of labor cost competition is the unit labor cost, driving for its attain-
ment puts the organized system at a comparative disadvantage.
Consequently, the effort to "take wages out of competition" through
collective bargaining eventually generates unemployment, and this
string of events provides leverage for the nonunion firms' wage and
employment policies in the local labor market. The unions do have the
power to raise wages above competitive levels (as distinct from taking
wages out of competition), and this provides another wedge for
nonunionism because it, too, generates unemployment. Nonunion
workers are aware of the unemployment tradeoff as well as the higher
union scale, and that factor affects their attitudes toward joining unions.

While it is demonstrable that unions and bargaining do raise
members' wages over comparable nonunion workers, even this is
overstated. Some of the union advantage must be attributed to what
Adam Smith identified as "compensating differentials," that is,
additional pay for working under difficult working conditions, such
as an assembly line and in other workplaces that are often unionized. In addition, employers' monopolistic powers in product markets (automobiles, steel, and aircraft production) have enabled them
to pay compensation above market levels, continuing a practice
that prevailed before these companies were organized. Protectionist trade policies have also aided union wage scales in such industries as auto manufacturing, and steel.

Imitative or Innovative?

Developments in nonunion labor relations are typically explained
by labor economists, at times joined by some nonunion employers,

as merely imitative of the bargaining system (the spillover or threat effect). The motive of the imitation, it is argued, is union avoidance. In addition to the "union avoidance" argument, the imitative/ threat effect to the nonunion system has been based on the belief that employers "buy" individual representation through matching or surpassing union compensation. Even if true, does this not match the unions' campaigns in organizing the unorganized by promising higher wage scales? The competition between union and nonunion systems is a serious contest between rivals regularly characterized by campaign rhetoric, akin to that in political contests. Many nonunion employers contend that their employees' annual earnings are greater than those of comparable unionized employees because of profit sharing and steadier employment, without the costs of union membership and loss of income from strikes.

The imitative sequence has been reinforced by those nonunion employers who accept the validity of the union spillover threat effect on the nonunion system. They obfuscate or fail to understand labor market processes and regard their own practices as a form of "me-too-ism." However, a reverse sequence in labor practices between the two systems began to surface in the 1980s. Some labor economists, whose support for the bargaining system cannot be doubted, acknowledge that developments in the system beyond collective bargaining became innovative. In fact, they went further and asserted that the imitative procedure was reversed at times, with the organized system imitating the nonunion system. As Kochan, Katz and McKersie wrote:

> We have traditionally studied the spillover effects of unions on unorganized workers and employers, noting . . . that the threat of becoming organized led many employers to match union wage gains and employment practices. Yet in recent years there have been numerous indications the causal flow has been reversed. Innovations in human resource management practices that started in nonunion firms are increasingly being carried over into unionized workplaces. (Kochan, Katz, and McKersie 1986, p. 9)

Some innovative practices of the nonunion model—flexible work systems and extensive employee communications and involvement programs—are unlikely to be transferred to the organized model, as data on unions' impact on the efficiency of firms in this country demonstrate (Hirsch 1991; 1997).

The two systems of industrial relations influence one another, but their fundamental relationship is competitive. And the acceleration of a market competition worldwide over the past several decades has sharpened the competition between them. The individual system has thrived in the more competitive environment; in contrast, the organized system has wilted. Academic specialists agree that what they termed the "New Deal" system of industrial relations, that is, the collective bargaining system, has succumbed to "changes in the economic environment [i.e., competition]. [And] even more important . . . the development of a nonunion industrial relations system as an alternative to the traditional model" (Kochan, Katz, and McKersie 1986, p. 46). They date the peak of the "traditional," or organized, industrial relations system in the mid-1950s, corresponding to my statistical finding, which dates the peak of the organized system in 1953, as noted earlier.

The International Decline of the Organized System and Responses to It

Just as many had expected a continued expansion of organized representation in the United States in the post–World War years, others anticipated a worldwide expansion of unionism. (Kerr, Dunlop, Harbison, and Myers 1960). A decade or so later, however, the organized private sector declined across all Group of 7 (G-7) countries, with the United States leading the way.

The response of the labor relations systems of other countries has varied, but in Europe works' councils became integrated with union representation and bargaining. Although both union and nonunion workers participate in the operations of works' councils, large numbers of workers do not belong to the unions. The councils are structures of employee participation in the workplace established by law, while unions have a different origin. Typically, unions negotiate the industry standards, while the works' councils handle local terms. In a fundamental way, therefore, works' councils have become substitutes for local unions and bargaining at the enterprise level. (Wever 1995). The two institutions can be at odds on this and in other ways. Their relationships are often adversarial, and the friction between them is likely to gather momentum as mergers and competitively driven downsizing in Europe take their toll of employment and unions. Global competition will likely exacerbate the relations between works' councils and unions in Europe, just as it has between individual and organized representation in the United States. If works' councils increasingly do become substitutes for unions, as unionism declines in Europe, the substitution would pose an unexpected challenge to advocates of similar structures for American labor relations. In the United States, advocates of works' councils (Weiler, 1990; Freeman and Rogers, 1993) believe such structures are not substitutes but incubators of organized representation.

A nonunion system, perhaps somewhat between the American and continental systems of industrial relations, is the British. This is suggested by the development of a practice known as derecognition. Derecognition is similar to a NLRB election for decertification. Beginning in the 1980s, the procedure permits employers to withdraw recognition from a union when they have reason to believe the membership of a union is no longer representative of employees. Unions may contest the employers' decision, and a government-conducted election will determine the outcome. There are also varying degrees of derecognition, ranging from total to partial derecognition. The point is that organized British workers now have an opportunity to select an alternative to the organized bargaining system in industrial relations.

The number and scope of derecognition have been small to date, but are significant given that it is taking place in the homeland of trade unionism. It represents a straw in the wind because the reasons for derecognition would be familiar to those conversant with the nonunion industrial relations system in the United States: "The most common external influence [for derecognition] was increased competition in product markets" (Claydon 1989, p. 217). Derecognition is dependent primarily on the strength of the union. Given the attrition of membership in Britain, the base for contesting derecognition has declined. While derecognition has been small in number (like decertification in the United States), the decline of unionism in both countries has been large. Nevertheless, the conventional view denies that the decline of the organized system has been coupled with a rise of a nonunion system in Britain: "The fall in union density since 1979 does not necessarily suggest a fundamental weakening of the position of trade union organisation within the establishment or enterprise" (McLoughlin and Beardwell 1989, p. 17). From a foreign perspective, this is a puzzling conclusion. One wonders how employee relations are managed when the majority of workers in a plant or company are not unionized?

The Plan of the Study from This Point

The conditions noted above as prerequisites for the development of the individual system—the wiping out of the pre–New Deal nonunion system, competition, technological change, and changes in the structure of employment—are examined in Chapter 2. It explains how they account for the long-term decline of the organized system in the United States and thereby create an opportunity for developing the individual system.

Chapter 3 considers the question, is the current relationship between the two systems a rerun of the era of the pre–New Deal years? The two periods have been invidiously compared, but I argue that the contemporary nonunion system is different from that of the past. Chapter 4 reports on workers' and employers' demands for individual representation, one of the conditions required for the system. Without the demand of workers for individual representation, would it be possible in an open society, the United States, for employers simply to impose such a system? Managerial preferences are a given and complement the workers' demand for a nonunion system, but I argue that management cannot by itself force it on workers. Given the fact that nearly 90 million workers in the private economy work outside unionism and collective bargaining, the population is too large to be treated as manipulated by nonunion employers. Chapter 4 also reviews polls of these workers as one basis for the existence of a demand for individual representation.

Chapters 5 and 6 address questions about how the individual system works. Chapter 5 reports on the links between the individual employee and management, including how grievances are resolved. Chapter 6 deals with how the terms and conditions of employment are determined under the individual system; it connects markets to the terms and conditions of employment. Chapter 7 asks whether there is a "third way" in labor relations. Some scholars contend that what they call the NER model is a system of employee relations (Kaufman and Taras 1999). However, the thesis of this book is that there are only two alternatives in employee-employer relations in the United States—the individual and organized systems—and that for the United States the NER model is illegal and therefore is not an alternative.

Another candidate for a "third way" in labor relations is employee participation plans, and they are considered from that standpoint (Chapter 7). I conclude that they do not qualify as a third way. Because of their importance, however, I review their role in labor relations. Employee participation plans apparently began in the 1970s and have since become a major issue dividing the two systems of labor relations that will likely remain contentious as the millennium unfolds. They were established primarily in nonunion companies for the purpose of increasing the efficiency of production, but unions regard them as obstacles to unionization. Paradoxically, participants in both systems of representation, independent observers, and a special commission set up by the Clinton administration to recommend changes in labor relations with an eye to the next century all concurred on the value of employee participation plans in promoting productive efficiency. For that reason, these plans are regarded as important to an economy increasingly engaged in worldwide competition, or what I call the New Age of Adam Smith.

The controversy over employee participation programs is whether they have a role in labor relations, a role distinct from their efficiency function. Briefly, this study regards the plans as efficiency organizations only. Nevertheless, unions oppose them because unions regard them as illegal labor organizations that deal with the terms and conditions of employment. Another reason, in my judgment, is that these plans strengthen the individual system. Nevertheless, there are some supporters of unionism who favor them as a preliminary step to union organization, but that view is not widely held outside academia. Meantime, some plans have been declared illegal labor organizations under the National Labor Relations Act. Major battles have and will be waged to redefine the standards under the act that would declare these plans legal.

In Chapter 8, the study examines the prospects for the individual and organized systems of labor relations for the next century. For the organized system, the question is, can unions make a comeback? My forecast is that, instead of a resurgence, the private organized system will decline further; by the new century it will shrink to 7 to 8 percent of the private workforce, or nearly the same percentage (density) as at the beginning of the twentieth century. Currently, the density rate is less than 10 percent. The negative outlook for the future of the organized system does not automatically assure the future of the individual system of representation. It requires, as the sufficient condition, that its key building blocks—the demand of workers for the system and a management that actively (and legally) supports it—remain intact. A declining organized system adds to the opportunity for the individual system, but does not guarantee it.

In the final chapter, I present the highlights and conclusions of the study.

——————— Two ———————

Setting the Stage for
Individual Representation

The Substitution Effect in Labor Markets

Competition and changes in technology and markets enabled individual representation to become a substitute for organized representation on a large scale. Over the long run, these forces reduced the organized system's share of the labor market (density) from its peak in 1953 to its present rate of just more than 9 percent, and after 1970, shrunk its population (its membership), from 17 million to its current level of 9.3 million. The largest of the labor market shifts is the continuing transition from an industrial (goods) to a service-dominated labor market. That structural transformation is sometimes referred to as the postindustrial labor market. It began in the United States in the mid-1950s and was eventually followed in all other major industrial nations. However, changes in employment were not limited to the broad shift from a goods to a service labor market. Occupational changes took place *within* both the industrial and service sectors of the labor markets, and these fostered the expansion of the individual system and the shrinkage of the organized system. The occupational changes increased the share of white-collar occupations—professional, technical, administrative, and managerial—most of which historically have preferred individual to organized representation, and reduced the share of blue-collar jobs, the mainstay of the organized system.

Structural Shifts within Manufacturing

The epicenter of the structural changes hit hardest at the keystone of the organized system, the manufacturing industries. They affected what was produced in manufacturing and the kinds of workers employed. High-tech industries grew rapidly as the older and more familiar manufacturing industries—steel, autos, and apparel—grew little or actually lost jobs. In terms of labor relations, the industrial-occupational matrix of employment became an exchange of unionized for unorganized jobs, and the individual system for the organized system of representation. The transformation was fueled by a continuing increase in global and domestic competition. Adding to the competitive pressure, during the 1980s the exchange rate of the dollar accentuated the decline of organized representation. Between 1979 and 1985, the dollar gained substantially in value against foreign currencies, with adverse effects for employment within the unionized manufacturing industries:

> From 1979 to 1985, as the dollar appreciated and structural change accelerated, U.S. labor resources shifted out of mature industries and production jobs most susceptible to import competition and toward the service-oriented manufacturing jobs in which the United States had a comparative advantage. (Little 1989, p. 68)

Not only did the newer, high-tech, nonunion industries maintain their employment through the financial storm, but they were even able to increase employment. Their comparative competitive advantage lay in their "heavy emphasis on managerial, technical and sales service" (Little 1989, p. 68), occupational groups that, as surveys of nonunion workers' attitudes and National Labor Relations Board (NLRB) elections show, prefer individual to organized representation by decisive margins.

On the other hand, the mature industries that were most penalized by the appreciation of the dollar were those in the organized system. Examples were autos, primary metals, apparel, lumber, paper, and leather manufacturing, all industries with substantial or appreciable measures of union presence. After the dollar turned down, the unionized industries did not recover their former levels or mix of employment, or their prior extent of union representation. Thus, swings in the value of the dollar had asymmetrical effects on the individual and organized systems of representation: under the same financial and international trade conditions, the individual system grew, while the organized system declined. Other short-run factors also diminished organized representation in manufacturing during the 1980s: the cyclical downturns of 1979–1980 and 1981–1982. Moreover, the organized system never recovered from the downturns in the ensuing upturns, while the individual system gained additional strength. Disinflation and competition spawned the 1980s' "give-back" phenomenon in collective bargaining, to the advantage of the individual system, as nonunion workers came to view the union as a diminishing and even a hapless giant.

Structural changes in employment are a long-term phenomenon. They are also a continuation of long-term cycles in industrial evolution. As economic development accelerates, the life histories of industries tend to become shorter: "An increase in the birth-rate of new products means an increase in the death-rate among old products and a decline in the average life-span of individual industries" (Mitchell, in Burns 1934, pp. xvii, xviii). In his study of the manufacturing industries, Fabricant pointed out that in "young industries, whose output shoots up quickly . . . employment [also] expands, most often rather rapidly." On the other hand, he wrote: "During the mature phase of an industry's development output expands slowly, if at all, . . . [and] jobs decrease unless the length of the working week is reduced sufficiently to offset the decline" (Fabricant 1942, p. 146). In essence, the life cycles of manufacturing companies and industries, while accelerated by events of the 1980s, were always present and underlie the long-run ebb in the organized system since its historic peak in 1953. Naturally, unions associated with mature and declining industries shared their fate. The impact of structural change is illustrated by the following roster of unions from an earlier age that were consigned to the "dust bin" of economic history: the Elastic Goring Workers, the Carriage Workers, Chandelier Workers, Straw and Ladies Hat Workers, Stogie Makers, Steel Plate Transferrers, Tip Printers, Glass Flatteners, Sheep Shearers, Mule Spinners, Cigar Makers, Broom and Whisk Makers, Tube Workers, Tack Makers, Sawsmiths, Gold Beaters, Pocket Knife Grinders. Our time has seen the disappearance of the union with the longest history, the Typographical Union. Many more have disappeared through mergers, and at this writing, the United Mine Workers, another union of ancient lineage is on the point of merger and disappearance from the industrial history of the union movement.

The effects of structural change on the organized system have been especially severe. Statistically, structural changes were found to be responsible for 72 percent of the decline of the organized system's overall market penetration between the years 1954 and 1979 (Freeman and Medoff 1984, p. 225). Measured another way, the broad structural changes would require unions to recruit more than 25 million new private-sector members while holding on to all 9.3 million they now enroll, implying a total membership of more than 35 million members, in order to regain their 1953 peak market share of 36 percent. That hypothetical population is double the unions' actual record high of 17 million in 1970. Such a population is today an unreasonable expectation among the leaders of unions and even among their most ardent academic supporters. Nor could the organized system recapture the more than 7 million members it lost from 1970 to 1998. It took private-sector unionism a decade from its low in 1933 to enroll 7 million members, and conditions comparable to those are not now present and are unlikely to appear in the future (Chapter 8).

Structural change impacted the competition between the two representation systems differently among the newly emerging labor markets. In the private services, the competition between the two systems has been moderate because these industries have always been mostly nonunion. The expansion of employment in the services brought about by structural change simply added to the sector's nonunion base. In contrast, the two systems compete most intensely in the industrial sector of the labor market, particularly in manufacturing. As noted above, manufacturing was the historic locus of the organized system, so any expansion of the individual system had to come at its expense. Moreover, the competition became especially acute within those industries experiencing declining employment and, therefore, where unionism was already on the defensive.

The competition between the two systems is best known by the term *employer opposition to union organization*. Contrary to the conventional wisdom, it is not a major explanation for the shrinkage of the organized system (Troy 1990). Moreover, the term is widely misunderstood, perhaps in some instances it is deliberately misrepresented. *Employer opposition, whether in the industrial or service labor market, affects the organization of the unorganized; it does not apply to the losses of the organized system resulting from the disappearance of bargaining units. These are brought about by downsizing, plant closings and the substitution of other goods from abroad or from the domestic economy.* The misunderstanding of what employer opposition actually means raises the paradox of why unions were so successful in organizing the unorganized during the 1930s and 1940s, despite the fiercest employer opposition of the century and probably in all union history, in contrast to their poor contemporary showing. Indeed, a whole new federation, the Congress of Industrial Organizations (CIO), was formed during those years, and manufacturing, historically mostly impervious to unionization, became extensively organized in the face of determined employer opposition. Obviously, something new has happened since those years. Employer opposition has always been an obstacle to unionization, and although it may now be more subtle, it is not, to repeat, the principal reason for the ebb of organized representation. *An important deficiency in the employer opposition explanation is the presence of employee opposition to the organized system. An unstated assumption of the employer opposition explanation is that nonunion workers will join unions if afforded the opportunity. However, there is a long-term trend in nonunion workers' rejection of unions, as is clearly indicated by unofficial surveys of workers' attitudes and the results of representation elections involving unorganized workers that are conducted by the NLRB (Chapters 4 and 8).*

Paradoxically, public policy as well as market factors have helped the individual system to take root and grow. In addition to protecting workers' right not to join a union, except under conditions noted in the previous chapter, the Taft-Hartley Act of 1947 has enabled employees represented by unions to decertify their bargaining representative. Employers cannot initiate decertification, it must be noted; but, employers can file petitions alleging a question over which organization does represent its workers, and seek an election to resolve the issue. However, employers must demonstrate doubt about a union's majority status. Quantitatively, the number of votes involved in these elections is small, even smaller than those in decertification elections.

Decertification elections require employees to challenge the union as their representative. Inasmuch as the challenge must be mounted by the employees themselves, the procedure is not easy to invoke. For that reason, and the fact that most union workers are satisfied with their representatives, the number of decertification elections and the number of employees involved is small. Nevertheless, these elections demonstrate that worker dissatisfaction with organized representation exists and has consequences. Such a demonstration was impossible under the original Wagner Act. Under that act, once employees chose a bargaining agent, for all practical purposes, public policy precluded a return to individual representation. Only through a logical fluke could this possibly have happened. Only if the bargaining rights of an incumbent were challenged by one or more other unions and all lost to a majority vote for no union could employees ever reject organized representation. Whether any such de facto decertifications ever occurred under the Wagner Act is unknown, but is unlikely.

Deindustrialization or Deunionization?

Because of the decline in investment and production worker employment in the traditional goods industries, some analysts termed the decline as constituting the "deindustrialization" of the American economy (Bluestone and Harrison 1982). The term is a misnomer. It implies a long-run absolute loss in manufacturing output. The output decline, if it were accurate, would translate into a decline of the contribution of manufacturing to the total output of the economy. However, the real value of output (the current dollar value of output deflated by price changes) originating in manufacturing has been stable over the last half century. The complex movements of the marked decline of manufacturing's share of total employment—the absolute decline in production worker jobs—but the stability of its share of real output, are explained by the compensating effect of the sector's gains in productivity. The growth of white-collar jobs and new products reflects the same complex forces. Such a performance can hardly be described as the loss of an industrial base.

But indeed there has been a transformation in manufacturing. Instead of deindustrialization, there has been extensive deunionization of manufacturing. But that has not come about from the ouster of unions. Instead, it has been the product of employment growth in the newer and other nonunion sectors of manufacturing, accompanied by the decline of the unionized sectors. Some nonunion companies in unionized industries have been undergoing rapid technological changes in response to global competition and in the process have either maintained or increased employment. The nonunion minimill steel companies are examples. The nonunion movement was also extended to the unionized auto manufacturing companies, all foreign owned. Japanese and more recently German producers who have moved to this country operate nonunion not only in traditional nonunion southern states but in Ohio (Honda) as well.

A comparison of union membership and employment in manufacturing demonstrates that the sector experienced extensive deunionization, rather than deindustrialization. Statistical data show that from 1973 to 1998, union membership in manufacturing dwindled from 7.8 to 3.3 million, a loss of 4.5 million in population. On the other hand, employment declined far less, from 20,108,000 to 19,961,000, a decline of less than 150,000 (Hirsch and Macpherson 1998; BLS 1999). This net result demonstrates that the decline of employment in the unionized industries was offset by gains in nonunion industries and companies.

Why the New Labor Market Favors the Individual System

The characteristics of the new labor markets differ between the service and industrial sectors. Service-sector jobs reintroduced the personalization of work, reversing the depersonalization that accompanied the switch from a craft to industrial production by the late nineteenth and early twentieth centuries: "Employees in many service industries are closely related to their work and often engage in a highly personalized activity that offers ample scope for the development of personal skill" (Fuchs 1968, p. 11). Those activities mesh with the individual system of representation. Concomitantly, the service labor market changed the occupational structure of employment, increasing white-collar employment and reducing the share of blue-collar jobs. However, the rise of white-collar employment in the service industries differs from that in the industrial sector. In the service sector, more white-collar employment required little substitution for blue-collar jobs. In contrast, the growth of white-collar jobs in the goods industries meant substituting these occupations for blue-collar occupations. Moreover, the rise of the service industries, particularly the health and business service industries, generated a new workforce with little or no historic association with organized representation. In the industrial sector, white-collar employees frequently worked in companies with a unionized blue-collar workforce; even so, they have not responded to union representation on a significant scale. While the relationship of nonunion white-collar employees to organized representation differed between the service and industrial sectors, both are predominantly nonunion, and so together they have sharply reduced organized system's market share.

Increased reliance on white-collar employment has raised the educational requirements for many occupations (professionals and technical groups) essential to private services, and this may be the most significant aspect affecting workers' preference for organized or individual representation. Greater investment in human capital is typically associated with a lower propensity for joining unions, again confirmed by official election results and polls of workers' attitudes toward joining unions. At the same time, blue-collar workers have also demonstrated their preference for individual representation (Chapters 4 and 8).

Structural changes in business organization have also tipped the balance in labor relations toward the individual system. The entrepreneurial structure in services, in general, is away from large corporate employers in the industrial economy to smaller-size employers and the self-employed. Services are characterized by smaller firms, often noncorporate, a wider dispersion of employment, and often owner-operated. Output is of greater heterogeneity than industrial production, and self-production of some services by consumers reduces the need for business production. This distances the worker from ultimate demand, a social and industrial gap favorable to the individual and unfavorable to the organized system of representation. The structural features of business organization complement the personalization of work and emphasize the close personal relations between the employer and the employed in the workplace, in contrast to industrial production and the organized system. Thus, they make private services less vulnerable to union penetration and more predisposed to individual representation. From 1990 to 1995, small businesses (those with fewer than 500 employees) in the service sector accounted for 85 percent of net new jobs. In general, small businesses accounted for more than three-quarters of net new jobs. They became more important in manufacturing and in construction, and less important in retail trade (U.S. Small Business Administration 1998).

Other characteristics of the new labor market that have advanced the spread and practice of the individual system are its greater reliance on employing women, younger workers, and part-timers (contingent workers), both in the service and industrial labor markets. This also further divides the organized from the individual system of industrial relations:

> The use of part-timers contributes significantly to the efficient operation of service firms because demand in many cases comes at

> particular hours of the day and particular days of the week. Given the
> importance of females, part-timers and the self-employed in the Ser-
> vice sector, it is not surprising to find large differences in the extent
> of unionization in the two sectors. (Fuchs, 1968, p. 11)

The postindustrial labor market has also fortified the individual
system of industrial relations by moderating the effects of business
cycles on employment. Because of this characteristic, the
postindustrial labor market has mitigated the severity, and perhaps
reduced the frequency, of business cycles. As a rule employment
in the service industries and occupations has declined far less in
past business downturns, and although downsizing in the 1990s
cut into the stability of some white-collar employment, the low
unemployment rate of the decade, as well as a historic opposition
to the organized system, kept this group from turning to unionism
for redress.

The organized system, in contrast to the individual system, remains more vulnerable to business downturns and downsizing because it is primarily in the cyclically sensitive goods industries,
particularly manufacturing. Within manufacturing, there is yet another cyclical divide favoring individual representation. The newer,
high-tech manufacturing industries are more resistant to business
downturns than the traditional manufacturing industries: "High tech
industries, although comprised largely of manufacturing industries,
performed better [with smaller employment losses] than manufacturing [as a whole] during [the 1981–1982 recession] (Burgan 1985,
p. 13). Because high-tech manufacturing is predominantly nonunion, while traditional manufacturing industries are organized,
market forces have steadily divided manufacturing between a cyclically resistant nonunion component and a cyclically sensitive
union component. Moreover, the cyclical effect on employment in
the unionized industries has not been symmetrical. During upturns
in the 1980s and 1990s, blue-collar employment and union membership in these industries, which fell during downturns, failed to
regain pre-trough levels. In effect, the cycle became a surrogate for
rationalizing employment, particularly organized employment. This
heightens workers' feelings of insecurity in employment and has

led workers, union and nonunion, to associate job insecurity with unionism, whether or not the association is justified.

Future Employment Trends

Long-term forecasts of employment indicate that as the economy enters the twenty-first century, the labor market can be expected to continue along the path it developed since mid-century. Between 1996 and 2006, the economy can be expected to generate nearly 17.6 million nonfarm jobs, almost all of which will be in the predominantly unorganized private services, trade, finance, insurance, and real estate. In contrast, the economy will add virtually no jobs in the more unionized industrial sector. In fact, manufacturing is expected to lose about 350,000 jobs. Much of the expected loss in employment will be concentrated in the union strongholds of steel and autos (Franklin 1997, Table 1, p. 40).

White-collar jobs, particularly administrative, professional, technical, and managerial occupations, will expand much faster than the average for all occupations; blue-collar jobs, skilled and unskilled, will lag well behind the average (Silvestri 1997, Table 1, p. 59). Inasmuch as total employment in the industrial sector will be at a virtual standstill, the net result means that white-collar jobs (implying nonunion jobs) will increase, while blue-collar jobs (implying union jobs) will fall in the industrial sector. As a result, the future labor market will be more dominated by nonunion industries and jobs than it is today. These projections reinforce the expectation that labor relations system beyond collective bargaining is likely to continue as the wave of the future, while the organized system heads into what I call a "twilight zone' (Chapter 8).

Competition and the Expansion of the Nonunion System

During the past two decades, both the union and nonunion systems have had to function under more competitive conditions than at any time since the emergence of the postindustrial labor market in the mid-1950s. In this new environment, the individual system, being innately better suited to the competitive world, grew; in contrast, the organized system, which depends on monopolistic conditions (Chapter 1), declined. Beginning in the late 1970s, under President Carter, competition within the domestic market was increased sharply because of the deregulation of transportation, communications, and public utilities. Historically, regulation was synonymous with the organized system, and such major unions as the Teamsters prospered as regulators customarily granted price increases to offset wage increases in the industry. In interstate road transportation, the Teamsters' membership plummeted, from a total of 2 million or more to about 1.3 million. The breakup of AT&T stimulated automation and competition in telecommunications and in the manufacture and service of communication equipment, and organized representation in these industries soon felt the impact in reduced membership and bargaining power. Deregulation, accompanied by structural changes in the furnishing of these services, opened these industries to the individual system.

Globalization of Competition

For a long time, America's preeminent position in the world's economy after World War II sustained the belief that collective bargaining and the organized system could insulate wages from competition. This country's predominance in the world's economy was enhanced for a considerable period because the economies of Western European countries and Japan were destroyed or severely damaged by the war and therefore could not compete. With the reemergence of these countries as significant and competitive producers, and a growing demand by American consumers for foreign products, companies could no longer ignore the relationship of labor costs and international competition. Services also could not escape the globalization of competition as American firms moved offshore to provide such services as airline ticket information, processing health-care claims, credit card applications, and the like. The Free Trade Agreement with Canada, followed by the North American Free Trade Agreement (NAFTA) with Canada and Mexico, and the approval of the General Agreement on Tariffs and Trade (GATT) put more competitive pressure on both systems of industrial relations, but the individual system, being better positioned to adjust to changes in how and what to produce in order to compete, has thrived; the organized system has wilted.

Responses of the Organized System

Can the organized system eventually adjust and cope with the new Age of Adam Smith, the postindustrial labor market, and compete with the nonunion system? The organized system has developed several responses, each dealing with the challenge of competition. One way was to adapt to the competitive conditions by concessionary bargaining during the 1980s; that has since been discarded. Labor-management cooperation is another. Yet another is industrial policy. During the 1980s, the collective bargaining system responded to the competitive pressures of the market with concessions and with labor-management cooperation. Although these steps showed recognition of the competitive world in the short run, leaders and members of organized labor lack a long-term response. Their short-term responses of concessionary bargaining got under way during the two recessions of the early 1980s and were designed to last until the economy recovered. During that time, give backs, wage freezes, limitations, and abandonment of cost-of-living adjustments, and departures from pattern settlements, became widespread. However, others interpreted these developments as fundamental and long-run changes in the collective bargaining system, not short-term adjustments (Freedman 1982). Individual companies and plants were found to be negotiating agreements tailored to fit their own competitive circumstances: "The framework is no longer follow-the-leader; instead it is the specific labor cost and competitive situation of the individual firm" (Freedman 1982, p. 16). Furthermore, Freedman argued that the changes in collective bargaining were permanent and that the future model of collective bargaining would not revert to the model of the 1970s: "We are returning to the individual conditions of the enterprise for good" (Freedman 1982, p. 17).

In the same vein, an expert from the Bureau of Labor Statistics (BLS) observed:

> The paramount issue in [organized] labor-management relations [in 1986] . . . was the same [as is having been] for several years—how to deal with the economic problems confronting both companies and unions . . . [that] the focus of negotiations was on meeting competition . . . [by concentrating] on ways to restrain labor costs, increase productivity and preserve jobs. New approaches emerged, and longstanding bargaining patterns disappeared as both labor and management sought to adjust to the shifting conditions in all forms of economic activity, ranging from individual plants to entire industries. (Ruben 1987, p. 37)

By 1993 little had changed in the BLS's assessment of collective bargaining and international trade:

> Management and labor negotiators continued to grapple with pressures to reduce or at least stabilize labor costs in the face of stiff foreign competition, the effects of deregulation in the transportation industry, structural and technological changes in many industries, and the spiraling costs of health care. (Cimini, Berman, and Johnson 1993, p. 19)

The business and financial conditions of the individual enterprise that collective bargaining needed to confront are already working ingredients in the individual system. These developments echo the finding in Chapter 1 that the market at times brings about a reverse spillover effect, with the unionized system imitating, or attempting to emulate, practices in the individual system.

Fundamentally, the organized system's slow adjustment to the new environment can be attributed to its reliance on a monopoly position in the labor market that is steadily deteriorating and past experiences, rather than planning for the future. No less an authority on organized labor than John Dunlop noted that unions are slow to alter their ways: "American labor organizations . . . are shaped much more basically by events of the past century than by forces of the past fifteen years" (Dunlop 1978, p. 79). The most current example of that rear-view-mirror outlook is the opposition of the organized system to fast-track approval in future trade negotiations, and its support of industrial policy. The essence of industrial policy is broad government intervention in the market in both foreign and domestic trade. Belief in that policy explains organized labor's opposition to a North American Free Trade Agreement and the General Agreement on Tariffs and Trade, as well as fast-track authorization for the president in trade negotiations. By favoring industrial policy, the unions hope to revive the strength of the organized system by shielding it from competitive forces. Analytically, from their perspective they are correct, but empirically, they are historically behind the times.

Another response of the bargaining system to increased competition is union-management cooperation. As a past president of the Industrial Relations Research Association, Milton Derber, commented several years ago: "I would anticipate some significant tilting [of union-management relations in the 1980s] in the mutualistic direction, partly because of increased trust between employers and union leaders, but mainly because of external competitors and conditions which represent threats to their very survival" (Derber 1982, p. 6). Another response to revive and strengthen the unionization of the workplace is by amending the National Labor Relations Act. Despite its obvious appeal, the record of union decline in market share since 1953 indicates that revising the law would not bring long-term relief (Chapter 8). Even more convincing evidence is the record of Canadian labor law and unionism. Despite a system of labor law far more supportive of the organized system than the American, Canadian unionism has not escaped the "American malady," steady and unremitting decline.

Meantime, industrial peace has paradoxically been another symptom of the malaise of the organized bargaining system. Collective bargaining was historically justified in 1935, in part as a peaceful substitute for employer determination of the terms and conditions of employment, work stoppages, and employer lockouts. Historically, strikes have been accounted a justifiable cost of the organized system in a free society. Irrespective of the merits of that policy, strike statistics over the past two decades show a marked decline, paralleling the decline of the bargaining system. There has been a conspicuous decline in the number of work stoppages, their duration, and time lost. In fact, the data record one of the most pacific periods in history of the organized system of industrial relations since the end of World War II.

The deterioration of the organized system has led to the question whether the bargaining system had entered a state of permanent decline. Not only unionists and sympathetic academics but also some management officials reject this possibility because they believe that self-interest would lead unions to take actions to blunt the competitive impact and reverse the downward trend in strength. In particular, they cite the election of new leadership at the AFL-CIO as evidence. However, this study rejects that outlook because a restoration of the monopoly market conditions necessary for the revival of the organized system cannot be foreseen. In fact, I predict that the future of the organized system is governed by what I call the "twilight zone" (Chapter 8).

———— Three ————

Why Contemporary Labor Relations Do Not Reprise the Pre–New Deal Era

The Issues

Analytically, and from a historical perspective, labor relations in both the nonunion and organized labor markets of the past two decades have been invidiously characterized as a reprise of the pre–New Deal period:

> Sharp and steady declines in unionization, experiments in union-management cooperation, [and] innovations in the work place [in the current period] would have sounded . . . familiar to observers of the American labor scene during the 1920s. (Jacoby 1986)

The presumed similarity also extends to claims that nonunion systems and the forces responsible for the decline of the organized systems in the two periods are the same (Dubofsky 1986).

However, neither the characters of the nonunion systems nor the decline of the organized system in the two eras are comparable. Except for international competition, the factors responsible for the fall of the organized system in both periods are the same: competition in the domestic markets, rapid technological advance, and the inability of the organized labor movement to cope with and to comprehend the new industries and labor markets (structural changes) that emerged after World War I. The American Federation of Labor (AFL) remained philosophically tied to the skilled trades of the nonmanufacturing industries of the nineteenth century, and if so was unprepared, perhaps even unwilling, to address the labor problems of blue-collar workers in the new manufacturing industries of the 1920s. The revolutionary new system of assembly-line production, notably in autos and related industries, was unfamiliar, not to say foreign, to the experience of the federation and its affiliated unions. What the unfamiliar mass production assembly-line industries, the "high-tech" industries of that period, were to the 1920s, computers, optical, medical, and communications goods are to our times. And the unions proved unable to penetrate the high-tech employments in both periods.

In terms of technological advance, the 1920s were among the most remarkable periods in the economic history of the United States, akin to the enormous technological advances experienced in recent decades. Domestic competition in the pre–New Deal era was fierce, as it is today; it was evidenced by employers' adamant and forceful opposition to the unionization of their employees. There were few legal restraints on employers' ability to resist and to attack efforts to unionize their workforces. In fact, the weight of legal intervention typically went against organized labor. In the contemporary period, employers still resist the organization of their employees, but employer opposition, as has been pointed out, is and remains a marginal factor in the decline of the union movement of recent decades. Instead of employer opposition, the main factor in the contemporary decline of the organized system was the sudden and tumultuous onslaught of the New Age of Adam Smith on the organized system. On the other hand, international competition played a small role in the fortunes of the organized system during the pre–New Deal era. In fact, America's trade and immigration policies insulated the organized system from foreign competition. In fact, after the adoption of the Smoot-Hawley protectionist tariffs in 1930, America virtually became a closed economy, further increasing the protection of the organized system. Currently, the organized system is vulnerable to international competition, and for that reason, it opposes efforts to reduce barriers to international commerce. Hence, the two periods are far apart with respect to the role of international commerce and therefore its impact on the decline of the organized system.

In addition to the absence of international competition, other factors in the pre–New Deal period have not been present in the recent period. To begin with, the character of the decline in the two periods differs significantly. In the pre–New Deal era, the decline was as rapid as it was precipitous because of two major reasons: the post–World War I readjustment of employment and depressions. The readjustment shrunk not only the bulge in employment related to World War I but concomitantly the union representation that had accompanied the expansion in jobs. The first of two major pre–New Deal depressions, and a short but a severe downturn in 1921–1922, also reduced the organized system, as the economy made its transition to postwar "normalcy." At the end of the decade, the economy suffered the worst depression in the nation's history, as monetary authorities converted what would have been a "garden variety" downturn into a catastrophe. These economic cataclysms devastated the organized system. Although the economy went through recessions in the 1970s and 1980s, they were not of the scope and severity of the pre–New Deal years, so their impact on the organized system, though powerful, was not on the scale of the earlier period. Moreover, a significant exception to general decline in unionism in the 1920s (until the Great Depression) was the *growth of the organized system in the construction industry because of a building boom in major cities.* In contrast, the organized system has made no headway in any private industrial sector during the contemporary period.

The characteristics of both the nonunion and organized systems in the two periods differ significantly. Nonunionism in the pre–New Deal era was conspicuous by its collective forms of representation, not by individual representation, as now. In the pre–New Deal era, collective groups, employee representation plans, joint committees, and company unions were hallmarks of nonunion labor relations; today, they are totally absent because they are illegal, and have been replaced by the individual system of representation. The organized system was the product of its own market power, by and large, in the years running up to the New Deal, and except on the railways, owed little to government interference in labor relations. The organized system of the pre–New Deal years was basically limited to a few nonmanufacturing industries and was made up overwhelmingly of skilled workers. In contrast, the center of the organized system today and since the New Deal has been manufacturing, and it embraces the entire range of blue-collar occupations.

The current system of individual representation is shorn of the paternalism of the 1920s; it depends on the demand of workers for individual representation as well as a management pushing for it. The Harris survey on behalf of the AFL-CIO reported that unrepresented employees go to their supervisors and management with grievances, both as individuals and in groups (Harris and Associates 1984). In fact, because these actions were so unexpected from nonunion employees, Harris cited them as a "glimmering" of hope for replacing individual with organized representation. Such has not been the case, as the record demonstrates. Instead, this behavior demonstrated the vitality of the individual system of representation. Harris's expression of a "glimmering" of hope for eventual unionism and collective bargaining echoes advocates of works' councils (or their equivalent) as a back door to unionism.

Communication between employers and employees differs radically between the past and the current systems. Under the welfare capitalism of the 1920s, the employee representation plan was supposed to be a means of communication between employees and employers, but in fact it usually was one-way communication, from the top down. This was an ingrained part of employers' paternalistic approach in the 1920s. In contrast, communications are two-way in the current nonunion system. As noted, unrepresented employees go to their supervisors and management with grievances, both as individuals and in groups. Such practices were virtually unheard of in the 1920s, or of limited value to the individual worker. The current practice was also encouraged by the current law, which states that individuals may present their grievances individually, under the organized system, only provided the union is made aware of it. Clearly, then, unorganized workers also have the support of the law to avail themselves of the opportunity to present their grievances.

Employee participation in improving the efficiency of the company is another important distinction between the contemporary and past systems of nonunion labor relations. Unlike the approach of the pre–New Deal era, the representative nonunion employer of today consults and encourages individual workers to participate in determining how the job should be done. Under the tenets of scientific management in the 1920s, "the individual workers were not to be consulted on how to do the job—they were to be told" (Perlman 1968, p. 123).

Another significant difference between the nonunion systems of the past and present is the scope of managerial authority. Managers in the 1920s wielded immense authority over employee relations. Since then, managerial authority has been greatly circumscribed by law and by practice. Employers in the earlier era could fire an employee at will. Employers could not only discharge employees for union sympathies but could blacklist any employee suspected or known to be a union sympathizer, and could do this without legal consequences. These weapons, together with many others affecting employees' right to organize, were struck down by the National Labor Relations Act. Limitations on employment at-will, together with other legal oversights of employees' rights, further limit the scope of managerial authority in the contemporary nonunion system when compared to the 1920s.

The evolution of human resource management has been another important development in managements' handling of employee relations since the pre–New Deal years. It is in large measure a response to the realization of the complexity of human relations, especially in an increasingly competitive marketplace. It is also a rejection of the traditional authoritarian model of management so characteristic of the 1920s and early 1930s. All the same, the substance of what is today referred to as human resource management is not a totally new phenomenon, as has already been suggested. Its meaning and importance were appreciated in the pre–New Deal years, although its practice was much more limited and differed from the present era. In the 1920s, managerial assessments of good human relations thought that "[industry's] most important task in this day of large-scale production is management of men on a human basis . . . that the individual employee represents a definite investment, and that sound business principles require that the investment be capably handled in order that it may yield a fair return" (Brody 1968, pp. 151, 153).

Employers' investment in the human capital of their workers has always been appreciated by management, but its view of optimizing that investment distinguishes the present from the past. The goal of contemporary human resource management is to open as many organizational functions as possible to employee influence and input, in contrast to the 1920s, while not abandoning its obligation and responsibility to manage. Today, employee input applies to the design of work, the leadership performance of supervisors, and the engagement of individuals and small groups of workers in workplace problems and decisions (Chapter 7).

Employees, the necessary partner to any system of industrial relations, have also changed dramatically between the 1920s and the present. The changes apply not only to a different industrial and occupational makeup of the workforce (Chapter 2), but most importantly to a widening of the horizon of individualism between the two eras. Growing adherence to the values of individualism is central to understanding why the nonunion system functions and flourishes. Under the industrial relations system, beyond unions and bargaining, competitive markets are the economic structures protecting the material interests of the individual worker and providing opportunities for individualism in the New Age of Adam Smith. It is a preconception of unions and their advocates that workers, if given the freedom to choose, will in most cases choose union representation. This claim is contradicted by surveys of workers' preference for nonunionism, as well as representation elections of the National Labor Relations Board (NLRB). For the 1920s, comparable surveys and government polls do not exist, but at least one assessment of that decade contended that employees' taste for individualism was a fact of life:

> There is no reason to believe that all workers are predisposed in favor
> of union membership . . . the important point is that unionism does
> not appeal to a lot of individual workers. Some view it as a blanket
> smothering the fires of their personal career ambitions. . . . Some feel

that the unions' omnipresent shibboleths . . . that what is good for the group averages out for the good of the individual, may only be correct in theory. . . . For these individuals, unionism per se is not good; and if the employer offers them a good personnel policy they are more than just satisfied. (Perlman 1968, pp. 130–131)

Apropos of that attitude, the ethos of the country differed widely in the two periods, as well, and this affected the public's and the workers' attitudes toward unionism. President Coolidge summed up the 1920s in the phrase "the business of America is business." In that America, unions were an "outside" force and were thought of by some as an alien, even radical (communist) force, as Sinclair Lewis's depicted in his novel *Dodsworth*. In contrast, today's unions enjoy a powerful position in American society, are courted by presidents and political leaders up and down the line, and can demand and frequently get actions from government to further their causes.

The most important difference between the nonunion systems of the 1920s and today is management. Contemporary management is a different breed from its counterpart of the 1920s. Not only is contemporary management better educated but it also has some two generations of experience in labor relations, organized and nonunion. One labor historian said that "management's education in employee relations was forced upon it piecemeal by its unpleasant experience with unions" (Ozanne 1967, p. 243). Management has learned about labor relations from experience, both on the job and in business schools. Contemporary nonunion managements often concede that unions made contributions to their understanding and handling of employee relations. Moreover, they are not ideologically opposed to the organized system as were their predecessors of the 1920s. Antiunion ideology in the pre–New Deal era, and the view that unionism was to be equated with radicalism, are not characteristic of contemporary management or, for that matter, of nonunion employees. Equating radicalism with unionism in the 1920s was an outgrowth of the Russian Revolution, and although there were examples of communists "boring from within" union movements, they were the exception and not the rule. Later, in the 1949–1950 period, the Congress of Industrial Organizations (CIO), under the leadership of Walter Reuther, a socialist, expelled about eleven unions from the Congress for being communist dominated. Today, ideological opposition to unions is negligible. Managerial opposition to unions is pragmatic, and motivated by competitive pressures. Indeed, management today does not argue that unions are innately "bad," as did their counterparts in the 1920s. Instead, they evaluate unionism as a net cost in the cost/benefit ratio of the performance of the company, and that is why they oppose unionization.

Paradoxically—and yet another dissimilarity between the two eras—the employer-initiated nonunion systems of the past had a more profound impact on the current organized system than on the contemporary individual system. The employers' nonunion systems in the pre–New Deal years were set up by the company; they were an industrial form of organization and representation unlike the structure prevailing in the organized system, which was based on workers' occupations. In the 1930s the committee, later the CIO, and its affiliated unions organized on the industrial basis, the same model employers used in setting up their employee organizations. Although the union movement was familiar with the industrial form of organization even before this time, the majority of unions in the AFL opposed it because it violated their craft principal of unionization. This difference led to a split between the AFL and the CIO that lasted until they merged in 1955. By way of a historical footnote, their merger never resolved the issue that originally divided them; instead, they merged on the basis of recognizing each other's existing bargaining units, a structure introduced by the National Labor Relations Act.

Until the industrial union structure was adopted by the organized system, manufacturing, especially such industries as auto, steel, electrical goods, chemicals, and tire manufacturing, had successfully avoided unionization. Clearly, the model and practices of the pre–New Deal forms of nonunion collective representation influenced the practices of the CIO and its new affiliated industrial unions. In fact, large sectors of steel manufacturing, communications, and communications equipment were actually examples of "organizing the organized," as former company unions were transformed into standard unions when they were absorbed by existing unions or when they independently staged their own transformation. Interestingly, this phenomenon of "organizing the unorganized" recurred and was a major factor in the rise of the new public-sector unions beginning in the 1960s. Some employee representation plans went in another direction, and instead of amalgamating with standard unions, transformed themselves into independent local unions. They borrowed on their experience as employee representation plans to withstand successfully the efforts of national unions to overcome them. Since these local independents are unions, legally and factually, they are also in competition with the individual system of representation.

Innovations of the pre–New Deal nonunion system of labor relations were also transmitted to the modern system of individual representation, to the organized system, and to current employment law. Along with employee representation plans, employers introduced an array of company-sponsored benefits, a package known at the time as welfare capitalism. The goal of welfare capitalism was "to attach individual workers to the corporate system by ties of "loyalty and dependence" (Harris and Associates 1984, p. 169). It applied to issues of concern to employees in and out of the workplace: housing, education, recreation, health, occupational safety, and economic security, and the conditions of employment (Harris and Associates 1984, p. 160). As it evolved, welfare capitalism extended its range of actions to accident, retirement, and death benefits; profit sharing; stock ownership; bonuses, savings, and suggestion plans; disability benefits; life insurance plans; paid vacations; and even guarantees of employment and income stability (Harris and Associates 1984, p. 169). Philosophically, welfare capitalism was paternalism in labor relations. Later, all its employee benefits became major terms and conditions of employment written into collective bargaining agreements and in the compensation package of nonunion workers in the individual system. Some were later enacted into law and are now part of the corpus of employment law. Because of its innovative features, the pre–New Deal nonunion system of welfare capitalism could have survived had it not been for the enactment of the National Labor Relations Act in 1935. One historical reappraisal concluded that "American industrial relations might well have continued on its paternalistic course" (Brody 1968, p. 178) in the absence of the New Deal labor relations program.

Some nonunion employers in the pre–New Deal era also introduced forerunners of human resource management and the "economy of high wages." Ford introduced the $5 a day wage in 1914, a high wage in its time, in order to attract and retain good workers. Doubtless, his opposition to unionism was a factor in its adoption, but Ford himself described his actions in words that economists find rational economic behavior:

> There was no charity in any way involved . . . we wanted to pay these wages so that the business would be on a lasting foundation. We were building for the future. A low wage business is always insecure. The payment of five dollars a day for an eight-hour day was one of the finest cost cutting moves we ever made. (Raff and Summers 1987, p. 35)

Did Ford's innovation succeed? According to an evaluation of that episode by researchers from the Harvard School of Business, Ford did accomplish his goal: "The increased wages did yield substantial productivity benefits and profits" (Raff and Summers 1987, p. 35). Collective bargaining later built on and augmented the high-wage practices established by many nonunion companies during their nonunion years.

Ford also introduced what might be termed an early version of human resource development early in the twentieth century. The company established a managerial organization to administer some aspects of labor relations. Among the actions taken of rudimentary human resource management were reforms to protect workers from arbitrary discharge by the shop foreman, although it is doubtful that these endured (Imai 1998). The employee representation plan, which was intended to introduce a two-way communication system between employees and management, was conceptually a forward-looking idea. In practice, however, it was a top-down arrangement intended to be a means of persuasion from above. Grievance adjustment was also introduced, but it, too, was flawed because employees had to take their grievances to their supervisors, against whom most complaints were probably directed, and who wielded the power to decide. Educational programs for foremen were introduced. Companies relying on their internal labor markets established job ladders and promotion rules. Improvements were made in personnel management, including the establishment of safety committees.

Of paramount importance in distinguishing between the two eras and their systems of labor relations was the role played by government. Until the New Deal, public policy, largely administered by the courts, went against the organized system and provided support to employers in their battles with unions. Public policy in the current period affects both systems, whether with an equal hand depends upon the viewpoint. In any case, the labor law enacted by the New Deal, albeit amended in ways opposed by the organized system and its adherents, remains a factor in the contemporary systems of organized and individual representation. With the onset of the New Deal, the visible hand of government became decisive in labor relations, and was decisively in favor of the organized system. Now, public policy augmented the organized system's own monopoly power and created a new system of organized representation, a system wholly different in kind from that which prevailed in the pre–New Deal period. And it is this system that in our time has withered under the power of markets and technological and structural changes in the labor market.

The Post-New Deal Organized System

The National Labor Relations Act of 1935 (upheld by the Supreme Court in 1937) and the policies of the agency administering the law, the NLRB, created a "new labor movement," one that was wholly different from that preceding the New Deal. Put another way, the enactment of the NLRA initiated a structural break in the forces governing the growth of unions (Sheflin, Troy, and Koeller 1981). The act spawned a new organized system of labor relations epitomized by the newly established CIO and a rejuvenated AFL. The new and revitalized unions and the NLRB extended the new organized system into sectors of the economy which had historically kept unionism and collective bargaining at bay. Employer-sponsored labor organizations that had been entrenched in these industries were eliminated and were replaced by the new, New Deal unionism. In companies and industries that did not become unionized, employee relations nominally were on the basis of individualism but, as pointed out in Chapter 2, were actually in a state of disarray that wiped clean the nonunion labor relations of the past. Nevertheless, a new system of nonunion labor relations emerged to compete with the new unionism: the individual system of representation.

Analytically, the structural change in the forces governing union trends became effective two years after the Supreme Court upheld the NLRA's constitutionality in 1937 (Sheflin 1984). The effect of the New Deal's labor policies lasted until the mid-1950s, twenty years, when another structural break, the transformation of employment from a goods- to a service-dominated labor market occurred (Chapter 2). This structural break, it must be emphasized, was generated by markets, in contrast to the government-induced structural break of the New Deal, because it exemplified the mastery of competitive market forces over the efforts of public policy to create monopolistic conditions in labor representation. In effect, the account of the competition between the individual and organized systems of representation ever since has been a playing out of the contest between markets and governmental policies, with the latter steadily and irrevocably losing out.

The arrival of the service labor market in the 1950s diminished the influence of the National Labor Relations Act (Keddy 1988). For the organized system, the switch from an industrial to a service labor market meant that the types of jobs that unions had finally succeeded in organizing and representing in the industrial sector of the labor market after two decades of the New Deal's labor policies were being replaced by jobs that unions found difficult to organize. In contrast, for the individual system, the onset of the service labor market and economy became a major opportunity, and the system began its steady rise to its present dominance in the labor market.

The origin of the contemporary individual system cannot be determined precisely. Although it is a matter of judgment, there are a number of reasons to argue that the contemporary nonunion system started in the mid-1950s. First, that dating is indicated by quantitative analysis showing that the structural break in the power of National Labor Relations Act occurred in the mid-1950s. Put another way, this meant that the power of the New Deal's labor law to foster unionism had decayed and was steadily becoming less effective, a development that continues to the present. (It is also the reason for continuing calls from the organized system and its adherents for "labor law reform.") Next, the statistical fracture coincided with the emergence of the service-dominated labor market around 1955, and with the historic peak of unions' market penetration at 36 percent in 1953. It was also the nadir of the nonunion labor market, as shown in Appendix Figure 1.

Development of the Contemporary Individual System of Representation

The contemporary nonunion system began, virtually, with a blank slate because of the policies of the NLRB since 1935, the activities of government policies during World War II and the Korean War, and the growth of organized labor until the 1950s. After the Supreme Court upheld the National Labor Relations Act in 1937, nonunion companies dealt with their employees on an ad hoc basis. Reeling from the impact of the new law and the unions' successes in organizing, most nonunion managements responded to the New Deal labor policies with a policy called "firefighting." Firefighting meant adamant opposition ranging from "no-holds-barred resistance" to legal procedures to ward off unionization (Nelson 1982). This meant fighting the NLRB in the courts, struggles with congressional investigations, and industrial warfare with unions. Firefighting was costly, but together with the resistance of nonunion employees to joining unions, the policy managed to keep most jobs out of collective bargaining.

However, market forces slowly began to undermine labor law and the unions by the mid-1950s; at the same time, they also initiated the development of the contemporary system of individual representation, and a new era in nonunion labor relations began to unfold. In effect, nonunion employer-employee relations were now also experiencing a "structural break" of their own, one comparable in importance to the one that created the New Deal organized system. The current system can be described as a new species of labor relations, a product of Social Darwinism. The process took much longer than it took the law to establish the New Deal model of the organized system because market forces operate more slowly than the application of public policy, and because the effects of markets are largely invisible. The appearance of the individual system was also unexpected because of a post–World War II belief that management had turned from opposition to acceptance of collective bargaining. Until at least the 1960s, even the AFL-CIO, influenced by these views, believed that employers had accepted organized representation and would not contest unionization as they had before World War II. This assessment was retrospectively reported as late as 1985 in the AFL-CIO's self-study of its problems: "By the 1950s and 1960s . . . to a large extent employers did not choose to interfere with their employees' exercise of the right of self-organization . . . [and] if workers chose a union, employers by and large complied with their legal duty to bargain . . . in an honest effort to reach a contract" (AFL-CIO 1985, p. 10).

If indeed this was true, it could have slowed the evolution of the individual system, but I believe that market changes, which are typically slow, and not changes in employer attitudes toward unions were responsible for the tardy appearance of the individual system. There is little doubt that employers had not changed their attitude toward unions, but instead had changed their tactics and strategies. It was also ironic because management had indeed become even more professional, as the AFL-CIO said, but its professionalism became directed toward avoiding unionism.

The structural break which initiated the contemporary system of individual representation was the product of markets rather than government policies. These were the newly emerging labor market, its negative impact on the organized system, managerial experience and knowledge about labor relations gained in the aftermath of the New Deal, and significant changes made in public policy by the Labor Management Relations Act of 1947 (the Taft-Hartley Act).

Taft-Hartley and the Individual System of Representation

While the original Wagner Act cleared away the old nonunion system of industrial relations, the Labor Management Relations Act (the Taft-Hartley Act) of 1947 contributed to the establishment of the new one. First, it shifted public policy from a one-sided preference for unions under the original act to one seeking a balance in union-management relations. Under the original act, only employers could violate the law. Section 7, the heart of the original and the amended act, was revised to state that employees had the right not to join a union, in the absence of agreements requiring membership as a condition of employment. This not only signaled a new departure in public policy but recognized that some employees did not see unionism and bargaining as the only alternative to improving working and living standards. The new version of Section 7 and the new nonunion system were enhanced in those states that decided to ban compulsory membership under section 14(b) of the amended act. That provision enabled individual states to override the union and agency shop agreements, otherwise permitted under federal law. Right-to-work laws facilitated the development of the individual system because by voiding compulsory membership in a union as a condition of employment, they assured individuals of their right not to be a union member. However, these nonmembers would still be represented by a union if the organization won the right to represent employees in a NLRB election.

For nonunion employers, the key element in the amended act was the protection of the employers' right of free speech. This provision protected employers' right to present their views on unionism and collective bargaining, provided those views contained no threat of reprisal or promise of benefit that could affect employees' exercise of their right to organize and to bargain collectively. Although there are conflicting views on the effectiveness of employers' right of free speech in representation elections, the free speech amendment clearly assisted the development of the new system of labor relations because management could express its views about unionism (and nonunionism) without violating the law, unlike the original act and as interpreted by the NLRB.

Another change in the law that assisted management in its dealings with employees under the individual system was the removal of supervisory employees from the jurisdiction of the National Labor Relations Act. For a brief period during and after World War II, the NLRB, after reversing itself more than once, finally decided to define supervisors as employees within the jurisdiction of the act. As a result, there was a surge of unionism among supervisors, in large part because the demands of staffing during the war led employers to promote many production workers, who were often union members, to supervisory positions. Management argued that it could not effectively deal with the production employees through another organized group sandwiched in between, and one that might take dictation from a larger union of production workers. Management regarded supervisors as the front line of management; if unionized, they would be incapable of carrying out top management's policies. Taft-Hartley, acting on this complaint, removed supervisors from the jurisdiction of the act. This change was essential to the development of the individual system mainly because the supervisor is the principal link between company policies and the employees. Looking ahead to the 1990s, the Commission on the Future of Worker-Management Relations, appointed by the Clinton administration in the spring of 1993, sought unsuccessfully to return supervisors to their status prior to the Taft-Hartley Act.

Another important change made by Taft-Hartley that made nonunionism possible was the decertification election. Under the Wagner Act, it was impossible for organized employees directly to remove their union representative despite their dissatisfaction with the union. Representation by a union, like a diamond, was "forever." Only in the unusual circumstance of a rival union challenging an incumbent union and in the ensuing election contest neither union won, and if the no-union vote gained a majority, could the no union choice of the employees prevail. The frequency of this development must have been nil. Under Taft-Hartley, employees, not employers, may petition the NLRB to decertify an incumbent bargaining representative.

The Individual System and the Public Sector

Will the individual system in the private labor market become a model for labor relations in the public economy? In the main, no, because government labor relations can be expected to remain largely immune to competitive forces, leaving little opportunity for the individual system to gain a foothold, even though most (more than 60 percent) government workers—federal, state, and local— are not members of unions. Should public education become a major battleground between private and public education, however, the individual system of representation could become a model for labor relations. I believe this is unlikely, despite the logic of the competitive forces at work. There could be more serious competitive challenges between the individual and organized systems in what I call the "quasi-public" sector, in particular health care, and public construction. Health care receives a major fraction of its income from public monies, and competition between public and private providers could lead to competition between the individual and organized systems of representation in the industry. Public construction could become a competitive area between the two systems of representation if the laws now favoring the organized system were altered to permit nonunion companies to bid and win contracts. Finally, should the postal service become privatized, a similar playing out of competition in how workers could be represented could develop. In general, however, the public organized system and the individual system will seldom compete in the next millennium. Even though most employees of federal, state, and local governments are nonunion, they rely on the civil service system, an alternative unique to public employment.

Although direct competition between the two systems is now and will most likely remain limited in the future, nonunion and unionized workers will be in conflict with the organized public sector because of a philosophical difference over the size of government in the economy. Public-sector unionism's goal is to increase the share of the national income spent by government, to redistribute more income from the private to the public economy. Private-sector workers, nonunion and organized, in general oppose that redistribution because it can only be financed by higher taxes and government borrowing.

——— Four ———

Preference of Workers and Management for the Individual System

Workers' Demand for Individual Representation

The preference of nonunion workers and management for individual representation is essential to the system. While managerial preference for individual representation can be taken as a given (Chapter 1), the demand of nonunion workers is either ignored in the literature or sublimated as a diminished demand for union representation (Farber and Kreuger 1993). It is not acknowledged as an independent determinant. Nevertheless, there is an explicit demand for individual representation, just as there is for organized representation. While nonunion workers' negative attitudes toward the organized system plays a role, it is subordinate to the affirmative demand for individual representation. Simply put, most nonunion workers want it.

The conventional view of the nonunion labor relationship is of worker dependency. However, this conflicts both with theory and empirical information. Workers' demand for the system can be measured in several ways: surveys and representation elections conducted by the National Labor Relations Board (NLRB). Several surveys of nonunion workers' willingness to join unions have been undertaken over the past two decades. In these, nonunion workers were asked if they would vote for a union in a secret ballot election or favor a union in their workplace. Workers are familiar with secret ballot elections because they are exactly the type that the NLRB has been conducting since its inception in 1935, and because they are familiar with secret ballot elections in the political process.

I begin with the survey of the Institute for Social Research of the University of Michigan in 1977. Nonunion workers were asked: "If an election was held with a secret ballot, would you vote for or against having a union or employees' association represent you?" (Medoff 1977, Table 4A, p. 10). Private-sector white- and blue-collar workers preferred nonunionism by more than two-thirds (67 percent): 61 percent of blue-collar workers said they would not vote for union representation, and a much higher proportion, 72 percent, of white-collar workers rejected union representation. Although these workers were asked about their preference for organized representation, their rejection constitutes a response in favor of individual representation. In the United States, there is no alternative form of representation.

The Harris and Associates study of 1984, which was commissioned by the AFL-CIO for its self-study, brought on by its awareness of declining ranks, asked nonunion workers:

> If an election were held tomorrow to decide whether your workplace would be unionized or not, do you think you would definitely vote for a union, probably vote for a union, probably vote against a union, or definitely vote against a union? (Harris and Associates 1984, Table 20, p. 63)

Sixty-five percent replied they would vote against the union, virtually the same proportion as the Michigan survey reported seven years earlier. The results can be interpreted in the same way: continuing demand for individual representation. Noteworthy, too, is the timing of the hypothetical voting. Harris asked if the election were held *tomorrow*, how would you (the nonunion worker) vote? Many critics of NLRB elections have argued that the time it takes between an NLRB order for an election and the balloting allows the employer to influence the outcome. This was the position of the Commission on the Future of Worker-Management Relations, or the Dunlop Commission, as well (Chapters 7 and 8). By referring to "tomorrow," the Harris survey eliminated the possibility of employer tactics delaying the workers' decision, a major criticism of government elections, yet 65 percent in the Harris survey said no to collective bargaining and yes to individual representation.

Harris also examined the nonunion workers' past history of voting in these elections and found that most were former union members. Of these, 57 percent had voted for a union in their previous work place. Nearly two-thirds of those who had never been union members said they had voted against the union in their previous workplace. Many of those who had voted for a union in their previous job apparently changed their minds about unions because just under three-fourths of all nonunion workers said they preferred their present job to remain nonunion.

Henry Farber combined the results of the Michigan and Harris surveys, and after adjusting for comparability (although I do not believe he adjusted for the public/private workers in the sample) showed that nonunion employees' preference for individual representation increased dramatically, rising from more than 60 percent in 1977 to more than two-thirds (67.6 percent) in 1984 (Farber 1989, p. 10). Later, Farber and Kreuger reported a continuation in the rising demand for individual representation or, as they put it, a continuing decline in the demand for union representation (Farber and Kreuger 1992, Abstract).

The union rejection rate (or pro individual representation rate) would have been higher in these surveys because public workers, who were included, have a much higher propensity to belong to unions than private-sector workers (Hills 1985). Currently, government workers' propensity to join unions is almost four times as great as in the private sector, as reflected in their respective market shares. In the public sector it is 37 percent, compared to just over 9 percent of private workers. The 1980 National Longitudinal Survey of men found that public employees' attitudes are significantly different from those in the private labor market. Among men aged 28–38, the only group in which a majority (54 percent) said they would vote for unions were those in government. The higher propensity of public-sector employees to join unions is also the likely explanation of why minorities are the only demographic group to support union representation (Hills 1985). Nevertheless, nearly three-quarters (73 percent) of nonunion male workers in all industries, aged 28–38, said that they would not vote for a union in a secret ballot election (Hills 1985). The results of the National Longitudinal Survey reinforced other surveys on nonunion workers' attitudes toward joining unions.

That high figure of union rejection (or pro-individual representation) was repeated in a survey by the *Washington Post* published in 1987 (based on 1986 data). In that survey, the paper asked: "In the place where you work, if there were an election, by secret ballot, among you and your co-workers, would you vote to form a union?" Seventy-five percent replied no, and only 25 percent replied yes (Perl 1987). In view of these preferences for individual representation, it is remarkable that unions do not lose a larger proportion of NLRB representation elections. I examine the possible reasons in Chapter 8.

Until the 1990s, the surveys consistently showed that about two-thirds of nonunion workers reported that in a secret ballot election they would not vote for a union. In a May 1993 poll of the public and of union members, the trend toward nonunionism was attributed "to the desire of employees to speak independently from unions" (Penn and Schoen 1993, p. 5). The specific question to which respondents were asked to reply, was whether employees would rather speak for themselves than through a union. This echoed earlier findings explaining the demand of workers for nonunion representation. In a 1992 report on the demand of workers for union representation, Farber and Kreuger reported: "We find that virtually all of the decline in union membership in the United States between 1977 and 1991 is due to a decline in worker demand for union representation" (Farber and Kreuger 1992, Abstract). While I reject the finding as responsible for unions' decline, it reiterates earlier findings of nonunion workers' demand for individual representation (Farber 1989, p. 10). A 1994 survey included in the final report of the U.S. Commission on the Future of Worker-Management Relations, reported that 55 percent of nonunion workers said they would vote against a union, 32 percent would vote for, and 13 percent declared they were undecided (Freeman and Rogers 1997). Another survey, completed in 1996, reported that 55 percent of employed nonunion workers would not vote for a union, and so presumably 45 percent would (Lipset and Meltz 1996).

It is also instructive to take into account nonunion Canadian workers' response to the same question put to American workers: would they support or vote for a union in a secret ballot election conducted by the various Canadian labor boards? Canada is of interest because its workers are believed to be more union-prone than American workers, and because its industrial relations systems are similar to the American. In fact, Canadian labor law is much more supportive of unions and bargaining, so much so, in fact, that Canadian labor law is often referred to as "Super Wagnerism." The phrase not only acknowledges the American origins of much of Canada's labor law but also its greater encouragement of the organized system than the American original. Not only has Canada's provincial and federal labor relations law stemmed from American public policy but many unions headquartered in the United States, known as international unions, once enrolled large numbers of members in Canada. For those reasons, it would be informative to discover the attitude of nonunion Canadian workers on the question of voting union or nonunion. Surprisingly, nonunion workers in Canada rejected unions (favored individual representation) at the same rate as in the United States (Canadian Federation of Labour 1990). In February 1990, the Canadian Federation of Labour (CFL) asked nonunion workers, who came from the private and public labor markets, the following question:

> Thinking about your own needs and your current employment situation and expectations, would you say that it is likely that you would consider joining or associating yourself with a union or professional association in the future? (Canadian Federation of Labour 1990, p. 3)

Sixty-six percent replied no, and 31 percent said yes, results that virtually replicated the surveys in the United States for similar populations of nonunion workers. If the Canadian survey dealt only with private-sector workers, the union rejection (pro-individual representation) rate would have been higher. Furthermore, the inclusion of Quebec in the Canadian sample undoubtedly also reduced the union rejection (pro-individual rate) because Quebec is *sui generis* in the Canadian system of industrial relations. On the other hand, English Canada more closely resembles the American. The CFL, which conducted the survey, was made up of unions that had broken away from the Canadian Labour Congress, the Canadian equivalent of the AFL-CIO, in 1982 over a jurisdictional dispute and remained separated for about a decade. It subsequently rejoined the Canadian Labour Congress. The CFL was made up primarily of building trades unions, unions which were then and continue to be affiliates of the AFL-CIO.

Similar findings about Canadian nonunion workers were turned up by the Canadian Federation of Independent Business (CFIB), an organization of small businesses. The CFIB commissioned the Angus Reid Group, an organization specializing in attitudinal and other surveys in Canada, to examine the attitudes of employees of small businesses in March 1991. Employees of small business were asked: "Would you rather belong to a union or not belong to a union?" For all small business companies 57 percent of the employees said no, 38 percent said yes, and 5 percent did not respond. By size of company (measured by employment), there was an inverse correlation between preference for individual representation and company size: the smaller the company, the greater the preference for nonunionism; conversely, the larger the employer, the greater the preference for a union. In no size group, however, did a majority of employees prefer to belong to a union. The highest preference for unions (companies with 300 or more employees, the largest workplace in the sample) was 48 percent, and this was matched by 47 percent who said they would rather not belong to a union.

What accounts for the fairly consistent support for individual representation and the rejection of the organized system of representation in the United States? The conventional explanation is fear of employer retaliation. Yet, in the Harris survey for the AFL-CIO in 1984, fear of the employer ranked near the bottom of the list of reasons given by nonunion workers. In that tabulation only 2 percent of the reasons were "fear of employer retaliation." In the *Washington Post*'s poll of 1986, 62 percent of the respondents said that fear of employer retaliation was not their reason for rejecting a union. These findings are noteworthy because the 1980s were denounced not only by organized labor and sympathetic academics as a period especially hostile to unionism, but this characterization was also relied on by the Clinton administration when it came into office in 1993, and was a prime motive for the appointment of the Dunlop Commission in the spring of that year.

Fear of the employer was also the public's explanation for workers not joining unions. A Penn and Schoen (1993) survey reported that 62 percent of the public believed employer pressure was responsible for the unions' decline. Thus, while nonunion workers themselves attributed only a minor role to fear of the employer for rejecting organized representation, the public and others gave it a major role. Employer opposition to unionism is indeed a reason for the decline of the organized system, but despite its popularity, it is not the principal reason (Chapter 3).

If fear of employer retaliation is not the principal reason for nonunion workers' avoidance of unionism, what are the major reasons? Nearly 60 percent of nonunion workers surveyed by the Harris organization characterized unions as stifling individual initiative (Harris and Associates 1984, p. 11, and Table 7, p. 50). Even 45 percent of union members said the same. Furthermore, 78 percent of nonunion workers told the Harris survey that they believed that their employer was genuinely concerned about them as individuals as well as employees. Ninety percent of nonunion workers described themselves as satisfied with their jobs; 51 percent described themselves as very satisfied (Harris and Associates 1984, Tables 9 and 11, pp. 52, 54). And as for their treatment by employers under the system of individual representation, 57 percent of nonunion workers agreed that most employees do not need unions to get fair treatment from their employers. The same percentage also believed that their employer provided all the pay and benefits the company could afford (Harris and Associates

1984, p. 12, and Tables 7, 19, pp. 50, 62). When individual employees feel aggrieved, Harris also reported that nonunion workers actively use their complaint systems and often approach management as individuals, as well as in groups, about work-related issues (Harris and Associates 1984, Table 17, p. 60). Although a more current survey of comparable scope to the Harris survey has yet to appear, the continuing rise in individual representation, and other collateral information over the past several decades indicate that its findings remain intact, if not strengthened (Chapter 8).

One apprehension that nonunion workers do have is fear of "the union unemployment effect," and it is one of the factors motivating nonunion workers to opt for the individual system. To many nonunion workers, union advantages in wage rates are offset by the unions' unemployment effect. To many nonunion workers, the unions' claim of providing job security has been transformed into the association of unions with job insecurity. Actually, there is an understandable confusion over the term "job security." Unions have unquestionably contributed to preventing arbitrary discharge, and in this sense unions can rightfully claim that the bargaining agreement offers job security. However, the term is typically mistakenly equated by workers and the public with employment security. As used here, nonunion workers have come to equate collective bargaining with *employment insecurity* or, in other words, the union unemployment effect.

Trends in manufacturing unemployment from 1980 through 1999 show that nonunion workers were not imagining the union unemployment effect or succumbing to employer propaganda. The unions' losses in membership over the two decades far exceeded the decline in employment in manufacturing and in other unionized sectors. (Increases in nonunion jobs offset the decline of union jobs to a large extent.) As reported in Chapter 2, statistical data show that from 1973 to 1997 union membership in manufacturing dwindled from 7.8 to 3.3 million, while employment declined by less than 150,000. Major reasons for this are the higher costs of doing business under collective bargaining and structural changes in the composition of employment (Chapter 2). Comparisons of union and nonunion plants showed higher costs in unionized plants coupled with no evidence that the unionized plants could offset the higher costs with advantages in productivity (Kochan, Katz, and McKersie 1986, pp. 103–104; Hirsch 1991; Long 1993).

Managerial Preference Is Rational Economic Behavior

Managerial preference for nonunion labor relations is common knowledge, as exemplified by a case study of an employer dealing with both unionized and individual systems of representation that "given a choice, managers will always opt for a nonunion operation" (Verma 1983, p. 166). Although the preference is common knowledge, the major advantage to a nonunion system is unlikely to be as familiar. The most important advantage to the nonunion system of individual representation is the company's freedom from the work rules that characterize the organized system. (Work rules have been derided by the apocryphal query, how many union electricians does it take to change a light bulb?) The obverse side of restrictions on work rules is the greater scope of managements' freedom to manage what economists call the production function, that is, how to produce the product or service.

Instead of these factors, the common wisdom almost certainly would single out lower compensation compared to union firms, and while this is surely part of the case, it is only part of the explanation. Union work rules and greater freedom to manage are more important because these affect the real measure of competitive costs: unit labor costs. Unit labor costs take into account productivity as well as wages and benefits, total compensation: If a company has high costs of compensation and also low productivity, its unit labor costs are high and put the firm at a competitive disadvantage. If a company has lower compensation or even pays the same as its competitors but enjoys higher productivity, its labor costs per unit of production are lower, thereby giving it a competitive advantage over its rivals. Labor costs per unit of production are universally the real basis of competitive advantage not only between companies but between regions of a nation and between countries. This principal has been recognized beginning with the work of David Ricardo early in the nineteenth century in his theory of comparative advantage in international trade. Ricardo's analysis relied on output per unit of one factor of production, labor input, but the principal is the same.

As empirical studies have shown, unorganized firms are typically at a competitive advantage relative to comparable unionized companies. Consequently, nonunion managements' financial preference for the individual system is based on rational economic and business behavior. For that reason, there is nothing inherently wrong or unfair for management to prefer individual representation as long as it does not gain that preference through actions that violate labor law. Analytically, therefore, managerial policies in favor of the individual system are a means to an end, and that objective is the profitability and survival of the company. Business and economic analyses dictate that for firms (employees, management, and owners) and for the economy, the profit motive is essential to competitive success. In a market economy profits are the mechanism for allocating resources, including labor, its most important resource. As Nobel Laureate Paul Samuelson and William Nordhaus have written:

> It is important to see the role of profits in guiding the market mechanism. Profits provide the rewards and penalties for businesses. Profits lead firms to enter areas where consumers want more goods, to leave areas where consumers want fewer goods, and to use the most efficient (or least costly) techniques of production. (Samuelson and Nordhaus 1985 p. 45)

Nonunion managements regularly seek to communicate with and emphasize to their employees the need to earn profits. Though this fact of competitive life may seem a commonplace truism, it is nevertheless often ignored or downplayed until companies fall on bad times and must retrench, fail, or go out of business. Some nonunion employers rely on the employees' handbook to explain the relationship of profits to employment and the success of the enterprise:

> . . . lower priced and more products increase job opportunities and have produced in America the highest standards of living in the world. Profit is the means though which plant, equipment and tools are provided. Without profit our jobs and growth opportunities will vanish.

Unionized firms have also found it useful to explain the need for profits to their employees, although at times, unions, some media, and some in the academy have, for whatever reasons, equated profits with evil and wrongdoing, misrepresenting the role that profits play in driving a market economy.

Like the role of unit labor costs and profits, the role of customer relations also ranks high in the nonunion system. To skeptics, this may sound banal, but it is a way of expressing the economists' concept of derived demand, that is, that managements' demand for workers is derived from consumers' demand for the company's product or service:

> Our customers are the judges of how well we serve them . . . and to meet their demands and gain new customers we must have a group of employees who take pride in their work . . . [that] every employee's standard of living, welfare and job security are closely related to the welfare of this company.

These prescriptions are emphasized whether or not employees are in direct contact with customers. In service firms with direct contact with customers, employee rules of conduct emphasize the importance of customer relations even more. Stressing the importance of customers to employee relations is an important feature of the individual system. It underscores the economic principle that there is a direct link between industrial relations, competitiveness, financial health, and employment. Likewise, another important linkage between economics and employee relations communicated in company policy statements is that "a union, despite its promises, cannot create jobs." Customer relations also figure in how employee participation groups work (Chapter 7).

Although profits are the principal driving force in managerial input-output decisions in both union and nonunion systems, it is also clear that businesses, organized or not, take into account other goals: to be a "good business citizen," in relation to the community at large, as well as in relation to employees. These supplementary goals are particularly important to nonunion management in order to show that its preference for the individual system should not be interpreted solely as a means of maximizing profits.

Another reason some of the nonunion managements prefer the individual system is previous unsatisfactory experience under collective bargaining. Justified or not, these experiences have reinforced their preference for nonunionism. For example, some of the reasons nonunion employers have identified for avoiding unions, if legally possible, are the costly effects of jurisdictional disputes between unions; these leave management (and the represented workers) in the middle. Another reason is union apprenticeship requirements, which are often restrictive and interfere with work assignments, which may not be geared to the specific training needs of the company, and which may be outdated. Likewise, experience with strikes, especially when they turn violent, and union opposition to technological change (although neither universal nor total), is common. Luddism may have originated in the nineteenth century, but it continues to affect decisions to change how things are produced.

Although managerial preference for the individual voice in labor relations is derived from competitive markets, some specialists in industrial relations continue to treat the preference as ideologically motivated, despite the history of the past half-century and longer. Management goals and values are described as "philosophy laden" or "doctrinaire" (Foulkes 1980, p. 46). This characterization converts such terms as "union avoidance" and "union-free environment" into ideological fighting words that obscure the market forces at work. As ideological fighting words, they have a pejorative tone, and for that reason many nonunion managements shun their use. On the other hand, opponents of individual representation use them to castigate and denigrate the system. These terms are the other side of another fighting expression, "employer opposition," which, like "union avoidance," has taken on a life of its own, one independent of its underlying meaning—competitive pressures. Some managements counter with symbolic language of their own (that they are pro-employee) to oppose unionism. The contest between the organized and individual system of representation is regularly fought out in ideological terminology, just as political contests are, while the real battle is actually waged in the unseen hand of markets.

Not surprisingly, the ideological contest has been extended, or perhaps it even originated, in the academic domain. For example, an analysis of management strategies in labor relations during the 1980s claimed that "it is becoming clear that market pressures are not the only forces driving . . . changes [in labor relations] . . . but . . . that [the] most important of management strategies may be the decision to try and avoid unions altogether" (Cappelli and Chalykoff 1975, p. 171).

Ideology did play a significant role in motivating management in the pre–New Deal era (Chapter 3), but it does not do so in the current managerial preference for the individual over the collective voice in employee relations. Pragmatism based on market exigencies, not an ideological chorus of "union free," motivates the current managerial philosophy preferring the individual voice in labor relations. The pragmatic approach is characteristic of nonunion management even for those who may think in ideological terms. For example, in a case study of nonunion and union industrial relations, an academic voice friendly to the organized system found that the "company strategy is seen by the managers as a pragmatic adjustment to external environment" (Verma 1983, p. 163). The term, "external environment" is a euphemism for competition.

Managerial preference for individual representation does not imply perfection in employee relations. To quote an anonymous nonunion manager: "I don't think that our employees expect us to be perfect. I don't even think they always expect you to be fair. They do expect you to be sincere and to do your best. When they mistrust your motives, then you are in trouble."

Empirical Evidence on Nonunionism and Profitability

The economic theories of lower unit labor costs and profitability that underlie managements' pragmatic preference for the individual system have been tested by empirical studies. *In Labor Unions and the Economic Performance of Firms*, Barry Hirsch contrasted the economic performance of comparable union and nonunion firms using several standards: profits, investment in physical capital, expenditures on research and development, as well as advertising as a percentage of sales and the ratio of debt to equity (higher in unionized firms). He concluded that "the results . . . strongly suggest that union decline and increased management hostility have been in no small part the direct result of the significantly worse economic performance of union companies than of [comparable] nonunion companies during the 1970s" (Hirsch 1991, p. 123). Freeman and Medoff (prounion labor economists at Harvard) also reported that the representative nonunion employer who says that unions lower profit is "essentially correct: Though exceptions can be found, unionization is more often than not associated with lower profitability" (Freeman and Medoff 1984, p. 181). Further, they continued that "unionized employers tend to earn a lower rate of return per dollar of capital than do nonunion employers." Although they found that this was more accentuated in concentrated industries, profit margins were reduced in more competitive industries as well (Freeman and Medoff 1984, p. 22, 186). In the same vein, Voos and Mishel, who also are sympathetic to the organized system, commented that while "economists have frequently asserted a particular [negative] relationship between unionism and profits . . . only recently has there been much empirical research on this issue . . . [and that] most studies to date find that unions reduce profits" (Voos and Mishel 1986, p. 106). The measurement of the effects of work rules on productivity, costs, and profitability are indirect and perhaps difficult to measure, but their negative impact on profits is evident. Stock markets, which assess all known and available information on the anticipated profitability of listed companies, have also registered a negative verdict on collective bargaining and profits. Studies of this relationship found unionization reduces the prices of the stock of publicly held corporations (Freeman and Medoff 1984, p. 184). Quantitative accounts of the effects of the organized system on privately held companies would doubtless reflect the same relationship.

When it comes to productivity levels and growth, the most important ingredients to a successful economic performance by firms, workers, and the economy, Hirsch concluded, are "neither theory or previous evidence provides unambiguous predictions as to union effects on productivity and productivity growth" (Hirsch 1991, p. 117) because the link of the organized system to the growth of productivity is "opaque." But Hirsch also stated that "even if unionism has no direct effect on productivity growth, it may affect it indirectly via its effects on growth-enhancing investments in physical and R&D capital" (Hirsch 1991, p. 5). To me, the relationship of growth in productivity and collective bargaining (work rules) is not opaque, as evidenced not only by the findings on profit but also by increased capital investments.

Freeman and Medoff contended that productivity levels are higher in unionized firms, but concluded that there is no empirical evidence that unionization affects the growth of productivity (Freeman and Medoff 1984, pp. 180, 170). Other studies found that productivity is reduced in unionized plants, especially older ones, and that their productivity rates did not offset higher labor costs in unionized plants (Kochan, Katz, and McKersie 1986, pp. 104, 106). If levels of productivity are higher in union firms (a matter of dispute, as Freeman and Medoff concede), the level (as distinct from the trend) of productivity can most likely be attributed to the history of companies involved. In short, the firms that had histories of high levels of productivity continued to experience high, but probably diminished, levels of productivity after being organized. Their postunion levels of efficiency, if still in place, are owed to their previous history of nonunionism.

This behavior is paralleled by the wage history of these companies, that is, they paid higher wages before their unionization, and after becoming part of the organized system, they continued to pay higher wages compared to nonunion firms. Subsequent unionization doubtless increased their wage levels over nonunion employers. At the same time, these higher wage levels, uncompensated by comparable gains in efficiency, also induced the displacement— the unemployment—of many former unionized employees. As previously noted, in some industries, many companies historically paid above-market rates to attract and retain the better workers, a practice that economists (in tune with business practices) have long recognized as "the economy of high wages."

When comparable organized and nonunion firms are examined with respect to employment, investigators in the United States and Britain found that "union firms had significantly slower employment growth than nonunion firms" (Long 1993, p. 693). Long's study on Canada for the years 1980–1985 found that "union firms in both the manufacturing and nonmanufacturing sectors experienced substantially lower employment growth than comparable nonunion firms . . . [although] small firms in both sectors . . . appeared to have escaped any negative union effect on employment growth" (Long 1993, p. 691).

Other studies also confirm the anticipated and actual experience of the greater flexibility in work assignments (restricted by union work rules), unit labor costs, and their effects on profits in nonunion compared to unionized firms. In a comparison of the industrial relations performance of the unorganized to organized systems it was found that "the design of the nonunion systems offers greater flexibility in the management and allocation of human resources . . . [that] on average [the nonunion systems] have lower labor costs . . . and [that] the magnitude of observed [union] cost differentials appear to be large enough to make the union plants less profitable" (Kochan, Katz, and McKersie 1986, pp. 107–108). The efficient allocation of resources, labor, capital, and raw materials is, of course, the core issue in economics. It is no less the economic rationale underlying the individual system of labor relations, as argued here.

Employers who have dealt with union work rules and their impact on productivity declare that union work rules and their effects on efficiency are neither opaque nor ambiguous: unions reduce efficiency. Indeed, when informed that some academics contend either that unions enhance productivity or that their statistical results are ambiguous, these employers are incredulous. If the academics' findings were reliable, they say, employers would petition unions to organize their employees.

Profits are affected by more than the direct unit labor costs under collective bargaining. Other features of bargaining, notably grievances culminating in arbitration and strikes, also raise unit costs of production. Analysis of the effect of grievances on costs and lower profitability in unionized firms found that "output losses associated with high grievance . . . rates [under collective bargaining] have substantial effects on profits . . . [and that] the average level of grievances was estimated to reduce profits in a mill by approximately 15 percent" (Kochan, Katz, and McKersie 1986, p. 93). Managements of nonunion companies believe that arbitration raises costs for other reasons as well. It turns over decisions to third parties, which deal with "employment rights," a wide, perhaps boundless domain, and ignores the connection between rights and costs. While not discounting the principle of impartiality, management believes that arbitrators' knowledge of the internal working conditions can only be sketchy, and so their awards frequently lead to inefficiencies and increased costs. The arbitration process is often lengthy, and its procedural aspects and awards can be subject to court review and enforcement, further prolonging the process and increasing the costs of doing business. In carrying out their duties, arbitrators see the impact of their actions as "micro," not systemic or "macro," in repercussions, but of course, as is well known to arbitrators, their decisions establish precedents, which have macro consequences. The arbitrator does not see a worker as part of a system of production, and so, as data on dismissals show, arbitrators restore many workers to their jobs, many of whom would probably be discharged for cause in the absence of arbitration. Because the impact of an arbitrator's award can and often does go beyond the case in question and affect the firm and therefore the rest of the employees through unemployment and higher prices to consumers, nonunion employers overwhelmingly, but not universally, reject arbitration in their complaint system.

Work stoppages—strikes—are an important cost of collective bargaining, and these costs are not only measured by foregone output and income but also by damaged customer relations because the future reliability of the firm to fulfill deliveries becomes questionable. This was forcefully demonstrated by the Teamsters' strike against the United Parcel Service (UPS) in 1997. As a result of the strike, the company lost business and naturally (because of the economic law of derived demand) reduced employment. Because of diminished sales, UPS also found itself unable to fulfill its contingent agreement of increasing the number of full-time employees.

The nonunion system avoids these costs, which reinforce nonunion managements' motives for preferring the individual system.

In contrast to the collective voice in the organized system, the individual voice facilitates flexibility in the utilization of human capital and is therefore more consistent with the goals of maximizing productivity, growth, wages, and company earnings. While the individual system increases the flexibility in managerial direction of its workforce in the assignment of tasks, it does not entirely eliminate work rules. Work rules are chiefly associated with the organized system, but industrial studies have shown that even in the absence of collective bargaining workplaces do have work rules. The employee participation programs seek to redress such practices (Chapter 7).

Individual workers' voice (at times called exit-entry), which is quitting and going to another employer, contributes to rational employer behavior. Although competition is imperfect in labor markets, competition does exist, and it still affords individuals the choice of quitting and going to another employer as a response to capriciousness or abuse. Historically, the conventional wisdom has emphasized the misdeeds of employers as characteristic of the non-union system, although the turnover experience of employees suggests a contrary conclusion. The individual exit-voice is neither toothless nor an oxymoron; it can impose costs on an abusive or exploitive employer, most notably the loss of the capital invested in the employee, especially that human capital which is employer specific. Put another way, would rational employers willfully damage their physical capital in an irrational fit of anger? If the latter behavior is irrational, how much more irrational would be the maltreatment of companies' most valuable resource, the employees who embody human capital, much of it the result of the employers' specific investment in their workers, putting aside moral or other values? In addition, the company's own employee practices, the company's complaint system, the law, the threat of unionism, as well as the freedom of workers to quit, are countervailing factors. Strikes in the organized system are customarily cited as the ultimate sanction to the superior power of the employer, but the number of strikes has declined sharply over the past two decades, indicating the weakening power of that sanction.

Members of unions may have less exit-voice with respect to their unions because of union shop (compulsory membership) agreements. Only as a result of the Taft-Hartley's amendment of such agreements can unions not demand that an employer discharge a member for any reason other than the nonpayment of regular dues or fees. Prior to that change in the law, unions could demand and get the discharge of a member declared not in good standing for any reason, no matter how capricious or false. In the organized system, members may be abused or worse because of corruption, violence, and criminality associated with some major unions. In collective bargaining, unions have sacrificed the interests of groups of skilled workers for "the greater good of the union as a whole," contradicting the academic assumption that the collective voice of "a union can take into account the desires of all workers in determining its demands at the bargaining table" (Freeman and Medoff 1984, p. 10). Moreover, such practices threaten a union's stability for reasons explained by Sidney and Beatrice Webb, chroniclers of British trade unionism. Nearly eighty years ago they wrote:

> Finally, experience seems to show that in no trade will a well-paid and well-organised but numerically weak section permanently consent to remain in subordination to inferior operatives, which any amalgamation of sections of a large and varied industry must usually involve (Webb and Webb 1920, p. 129)

In updated American terminology, the Webbs pointed to the instability of combining skilled union workers with unskilled members into a single industrial unit because, for political reasons, the union leadership will sacrifice the interests of the numerically smaller skilled to the interests of the larger, unskilled members. As previously noted, this issue divided the AFL and the CIO in the 1930s. Their merger in 1955 never resolved the issue; instead, each reciprocally recognized the bargaining units that affiliates had organized under the National Labor Relations Act. In bargaining, and just as the Webbs had foreseen, industrial unions were eventually forced to give their skilled members a veto power over all contracts to prevent the exploitation of the numerically smaller skilled trades and to avert their secession from the union. Thus, as the

Webbs foresaw, in the mid-1950s a group of skilled workers threatened to secede from the United Auto Workers because successive contracts had compressed the skilled workers' wage differentials. Only when the union agreed to renegotiate the agreement that finally precipitated the revolt, and agreed to a permanent change in the union's constitution setting up a skilled trades department with the right to veto future agreements affecting skill differentials, did the movement to secede end. Similar developments occurred among one or more industrial unions (Troy 1960).

The Population of Companies and Nonunionism

Because of the large number of companies in the American economy, the individual system has an inherent advantage over the organized system in presenting numerous choices to the worker. The large number of enterprises also confronts unions with the challenge of who to organize. Over 3 million corporations file tax returns with the IRS, the number of individual nonfarm proprietorships filing returns is almost 17 million, and there are about 1.7 million partnerships. Given so many businesses, the individual worker has a wide range of employers to validate his exit-voice. As for union organizing, even eliminating many firms as probably too small to be meaningful, the unions' task of tracking and organizing so many businesses, even if limited to the "strategically" important ones, has to be formidable, if not impossible. Meanwhile, the number of businesses has increased considerably over the past half century, while the number of labor organizations, as well as their membership in the private economy, has declined sharply. The peak population of union organizations—locals, intermediates, national and international unions—was about 50,000, and that was more than forty years ago. Currently, there are perhaps 30,000 in the private economy. The dwindling population of union organizations handicaps their organizing and, conversely, promotes the growth and viability of the nonunion system. In addition, given that small businesses have generated most of the growth in employment over the recent past, the growth of the individual system, by derivation, is enhanced.

The decentralization of the nonunion system facilitates variation in employer techniques and innovations in labor relations. Decentralization in the nonunion system applies to multiplant companies as well as to individual companies. As in the organized system, where general policies are determined at the headquarters or national level, in the nonunion system corporate headquarters also establish the general policies, but plants and subsidiary units of a large company are given considerable leeway in the conduct of employee relations (and other matters); and they are expected to exercise it. Specifically, this means tailoring employee terms and conditions of employment to local market conditions. Corporate headquarters provides support, funding and "a little direction, if business is doing well," but if the "business is not doing well . . . we [corporate headquarters] become more actively involved." The exercise of managerial authority among the larger companies is diffused because of size: each location has a human resource or personnel office, while the division has one or more employee relations executives, and the corporate headquarters has a vice-president of employee or human resource management. This is so even in situations where corporate headquarters are in charge of major final decisions in labor relations. Policies set at corporate offices steer local management, but flexibility is expected of the local management within the operational instructions. This versatility makes the system of even large employers more flexible than would be expected, and less vulnerable to unionization. Associations of nonunion companies, such as the educational affiliate of the National Association of Manufacturers, known as CUE (the acronym for its original title, Committee for a Union Free Environment) disseminate information about nonunion employee relations practices and how to avoid unionization legally. In that respect, it operates as a counterpart to union conventions and special programs, often conducted on university campuses, on how to organize the nonunion companies (Chapter 8).

The unionized system is also decentralized: ". . . collective bargaining agreements tend to be comprehensive, and bargaining tends to involve only one tier of relationships, e.g. between a company and a union, or between a plant and a union" (Mills 1986, p. 14), but decentralization in the organized system is less flexible. Pattern bargaining and imitation of other union agreements as well as previous agreements constrain bargainers. Even though these practices are gradually eroding because of the exigencies of competition and the decline of the union movement, the organized system, because of its conservative nature, is less open to change in labor relations. Moreover, union mergers often bring together diverse groups of workers into the same organization, and this makes difficult the new union's understanding and representation of the special needs of its heterogeneous membership. At the same time, because the organized system seeks to generate uniformity in employment standards and in the treatment of employee rights, it can often be at odds with market realities. The outstanding example of such rigidity is the organized system's oft-repeated goal of "taking wages out of competition," even though the goal is unattainable. Very likely, establishing uniform wage rates in collective bargaining agreements across companies and regions is mistakenly considered as taking wages out of competition. As explained above, however, it is unit labor costs that determine the relative positions of competitive companies. Meanwhile, the pursuit of the goal of wage uniformity inspires a conservative and rigid stance at variance with the market and has doubtless been responsible for some unemployment among union members.

The individual system is also diverse because of the diversity of its origins. Simply stated, some are "ancient," while others are new. Although the current system and its practices are post–World War II, many companies and establishments that are nonunion today have always been so; some even date back to the beginning of the century. Their current practices, however, as are all those whose history of nonunion employee relations antedated the National Labor Relations Act, are totally different from earlier times. Another important source of diversity in nonunionism comes from new companies and new branches of existing companies. These begin with a tabula rasa burnished by a growing experience of nonunionism, provided by employer groups.

Management Philosophy

The management of nonunion companies has a philosophy of labor relations, just as unions do (Troy 1999). It is based on two principles: (1) a commitment to dealing with employees on an individual basis, and (2) an expectation that the employees also accept that belief. In stating that management must have a commitment to nonunion labor relations, I mean that token and fatuous lip service undermine relations with employees because its cynicism is quickly perceived by the workers. It ripens the opportunities for unions to organize a disaffected workforce. For nonunion management the core of their philosophy is that "both the company and its employees derive the greatest benefit from this type of relationship." The intent of management's philosophy is to emphasize mutual over adversarial interests. This is not to say that conflicts are absent in the nonunion system or that mutuality of interests does not exist in organized relationships.

For management, the application of its philosophy favoring nonunion labor relations requires a (legal) "hands on" approach. In the absence of an intermediary body, a union, management's dealings with its employees must necessarily be direct and must demonstrate a commitment to that type of relationship. Because its dealings with the employees are direct, the scope of managerial responsibilities in employee relations are greater than under collective bargaining. Simply put, there is a lot more work for management to do, if only because management's right to manage, which it prizes very highly, can only be given its fullest scope under the individual system. In contrast, the organized system automatically reduces the scope of managerial authority. In the nonunion system, management is expected to do in labor relations what the word implies in other domains of the business—manage. This said, the opportunity is not easy to realize. In contrast to the problems management faces in dealing with production, finance, marketing and research, those in employee relations are more amorphous and less susceptible to well-defined and optimal solutions. The reason is that employee relations problems are "people problems," and very likely, people with whom some in management must come into personal contact fairly often. Application of the "hands on" approach begins by informing individual employees that "[our company] recognizes your right to join and assist labor organizations of your own choice, and it also recognizes that you have a right to refrain from joining or assisting any labor organization." By using the language of the National Labor Relations Act, as amended in 1947, the employer is able, paradoxically, to reinforce its goal to deal with employees individually.

Although management's statements on philosophy and policy may be clear in intent, there are occasions when they are confusing or even wrong in expression. For example: "The policy of our company is that of an open shop. No employee need belong to any labor organization in order to be employed or to continue his/her employment with the company." Employees are then informed that the company's "open shop" philosophy should not be interpreted as an attack on unions, but "that the interest of all employees will be best served by working directly with each other rather than through outsiders." While it is literally accurate that individual employees may belong to a union in an unrepresented group, the company does not and cannot deal with them differently from nonmembers, which might be implied by the expression. Since enactment of the National Labor Relations Act, discrimination against employees for membership or nonmembership in a union is a violation of the law, unless there is a valid contract requiring membership as a condition of employment. Since 1947, however, compulsory membership is inapplicable in states that have enacted right-to-work laws. Under the National Labor Relations Act of 1935, and ever since, employers can deal only with the exclusive representative or, in the absence of a labor organization representing the employees, with employees on an individual basis.

Reference to an open shop in the current system of individual representation reflects an outdated concept from the years prior to the National Labor Relations Act. In pre-National-Labor-Relations-Act days, the company, if it wished, could deal with individuals who were union members separately from nonunion employees. Such procedures are illegal today. Perhaps the current reference to the open shop is intended to refer to those employees who are represented by a union but are not members under the legal doctrine of exclusive representation. However, that is doubtful. Under exclusive representation, whether or not an individual is a member of the union, the union represents all employees, irrespective of membership, and all are uniformly subject to the terms of the agreement. Strictly speaking, there is no such thing as the "open shop" in its historical context.

A more accurate expression of management philosophy toward individual representation is summarized by the following:

> We believe each person is different. Each man and woman has different combinations of talents, abilities, skills, energies, motivations, and ambitions.
>
> We believe each person wants and deserves to be treated on an individual basis. Individual treatment means also that each employee wants to be, and should be, recognized on the basis of his or her own accomplishments.
>
> We believe that everyone who works at [our company] has a common stake in our company's competitive strength, growth and success. This means that we want employees to be well informed as to what is going on and have a sense of participation in the affairs of the business. We know the company is strengthened when employees participate and work well together.
>
> We believe the best way to deal with the problems and questions that inevitably arise in the daily conduct of the business is for the individual employee to discuss his or her question directly with the individual best able to provide an answer. (In most cases that person is the employee's immediate supervisor.) We believe problems and questions are best resolved and answered in one-on-one, frank, and open discussion. As questions are dealt with on an individual basis, the employee acquires a better understanding of the business, and in many cases the employee can make a real contribution to the solution of a problem or the improvement of a policy or practice.
>
> We recognize a primary management responsibility to provide a high Quality of Work life for the employees. When people commit their talents, energies, and working lives to a company, we must do everything reasonably within our power to provide them with the

maximum job satisfaction, enjoyment, and pride in what they do. Where direct individual relationships are maintained, we believe the employee enjoys a higher Quality of Work life and derives greater job satisfaction from his or her work.

Each of the foregoing principles addresses different aspects of the system of individual representation. They may be summarized as (1) recognition of individual qualities among employees; (2) treating each worker, to as great an extent as possible, on the basis of these differences; (3) continuing and meaningful communication with employees as individuals; (4) a procedure to hear and adjust individual complaints; (5) management responsibility for good and safe physical working conditions to protect the worker; and (6) to enable the individual worker to optimize his/her employment opportunities.

To reinforce its commitment to individual representation, some employee handbooks often contain a letter from the chief operating officer or chairman of the board making clear that the company policy is supported from the top. Excerpts from such a statement emphasize that the company's success depends on "the performance and skills of all . . . employees" and links that performance to competitiveness "in today's worldwide marketplace."

The other side of management's preference for individual representation is management opposition to group (union) representation explicitly stated in employee handbooks: "Open and frank communication . . . can best be accomplished without third party interference or representation . . . [that] a union free environment is in your [the employee's] best interest, the company's best interest and in the interest of the customers we serve." The same companies that also may have organized relationships in other business divisions add that the company will make "every effort to maintain a credible, responsible relationship" with their organized employees.

The ultimate objective of management philosophy is to build employee loyalty. From the trends in National Labor Relations Board (NLRB) elections in previously unorganized units (Chapter 8) and from survey data on individual preferences, it is evident that this goal is being achieved. It is also evident that employee loyalty cannot and is not bought by the nonunion system. Where there are blatant efforts to do so, for example, avoiding suspensions of egregious employee behavior at all costs in an effort to discourage workers from turning to a union for redress, the result is not a gain in employee loyalty but disrespect for management as managers. Credibility, the hallmark of a successful nonunion system, is eroded by appeasement.

While management philosophy emphasizes the responsibilities of management, employee responsibility for actions is also part of the credo. Paternalism is avoided in the contemporary nonunion system. Paternalism, which characterized many nonunion employers' labor policies in the pre–New Deal era, has become obsolescent in the new systems of labor relations. A policy of paternalism would be an invitation to open-ended "greenmail." Likewise, compensation policy in nonunion companies rejects the idea that the relationship can be purchased. As for employees' responsibilities, management holds them accountable; it rejects the misconception, as some might believe, of accepting unsatisfactory behavior in order to maintain a nonunion status. It is not a permissive system. As we see in our discussion of the nonunion complaint system, however, there are examples of managements bending over backward to avoid disciplining an employee, but they do so at the cost of the credibility of the system.

Illustrative of managements' expectations from employees is that they

- Continually act in [the company's] best interest and strive for excellent performance in all they pursue.
- Act in a manner consistent with [the company's] primary values.
- Take primary responsibility for their personal growth and career development.
- Fully communicate with and utilize the skills, talents, and resources of co-workers in order to meet [the company's] needs.
- Seek out innovative opportunities to serve and contribute to achievement of organization objectives.

While emphatic in its preference for individual representation, nonunion managements agree that some employers do not treat their employees fairly, and for these workers collective representation becomes an alternative. This, again, indicates the pragmatic over the ideological approach to nonunion representation.

Managements criticize the leadership of unions on the grounds that they "tend to be guided by broad, macro considerations and by personal political power rather than the problems of the individual worker." In this context, it should be recalled that many friends of the union movement have also argued that the union leadership has often become remote from the membership. One analyst has contended that one way around this is to form local independent unions, a proposal that will find little response among main-line unionists (Jacoby 1986). Other nonunion managerial criticisms of the organized system are restrictive work practices which undermine efficiency, generate price increases, and weaken the firm's competitive position; and strikes, which injure the company as well as employees financially, and weaken the stability of customer relations. They also point to factionalism within unions over union-management cooperation, and to the fact that some committed unionists regard such cooperation as a contradiction in terms. For example, a faction in the United Auto Workers (UAW) challenged the leadership and the majority of the membership over cooperative efforts with management to improve labor relations and the competitive position of the unionized auto companies. The dissident movement, known as "New Directions," asserted that to be a cooperative adversary is an oxymoron.

Human Resource Management

The strategic planners of management policies in labor relations in both the nonunion and organized systems are human resource specialists. Their primary objective in the nonunion system is to encourage employees to recognize that mutual interests outweigh adversarial interests and that the objectives of the employer and the employee can best be attained through individual representation. The role of human resource management in the individual system is therefore greater and more important because, if their work is successful, the nonunion system will work, and unions will be kept at bay. Despite elaborate procedures, in the end the nonunion worker must himself want the individual relationship.

Nevertheless, it would be a fallacy to treat human resource management as but a special aspect of managerial opposition to unionism, the velvet glove over the mailed fist, and even responsible for the decline of the union movement. Many employers credit human resource management with holding the union at bay and with union decline, but both perspectives exaggerate its power. The failure of unions to organize and the decline of the union movement are the product of broad and powerful market forces, including employees' demand for individual representation. Moreover, if employees were to regard antiunionism as the "raison d'être" of human resource management, then the ability of human resource management to encourage employee motivation and participation in the working life of the company is diminished. One-dimensional policy will fail.

Nevertheless, human resource management doubtless has helped shift the initiative from unions to management in strategic planning in labor relations, particularly in influencing the demand of employees for individual rather than collective representation. To achieve its goal, human resource management strives to show the advantages of the nonunion system in both human relations and financial terms. It seeks to demonstrate that union representation is unnecessary, a goal that is already widely held by nonunion workers, as survey data have shown, and so human resource management begins with an advantage in this task. From this perspective, human resource management regards its policies as "proactive," in contrast to "reactive" policies, which are intended to head off the union when it appears at the company gates. The hallmark of pro-active policies is the company's culture. In a multiestablishment company, there are variations around a theme developed at corporate headquarters. The concept of a company culture, particularly in employee relations, is the company's equivalent of the differentiation of its products from other sellers. Like differentiation in the product market, the goal in defining company culture in labor relations is distinctiveness. While many human resource managements make claims of achieving this objective, and probably do, at times it sounds like a slogan. However, similar claims also apply to the organized system.

Human resource management encompasses personnel administration as well as employee relations. Its operational, as distinct from its strategic, responsibilities range from recruitment to working conditions, communications, and the administration of the complaint system. Human resource management also develops information on compensation, formulates and applies the companies' complaint procedures, and surveys employee reactions to the employers' policies. Human resource management in the nonunion system is essentially a staff function. The primary responsibility for carrying out managerial policies rests with front-line supervision.

Human resource staff constitute a key source (second only to supervisors) for assessing the quality of employee relations. Corporate- and division-level personnel are responsible for detecting problems in employee relations in their early stages, in particular the threat of unionization. The staff attends meetings with employees, checks into grievances, and is depended on to facilitate employee discussions of problems with management. To supplement information, the staff uses surveys of employee attitudes conducted either by outside professionals or the staff itself. Surveys are meant to learn what employees think in general, and on specific issues, to gain ideas, suggestions, and opinions about company practices and to provide a factual basis for human resource staff to make recommendations for change. Typically, surveys of employee attitudes cover employee confidence in management and supervisors, fairness in treatment and pay, pride in the company, performance feedback, and working conditions—including job content, work-group cooperation, promotion opportunities, opportunities to use one's abilities, and company benefits. The questions or statements used in surveys are written in simple English, perhaps at the level of high school or just below.

The Employee Handbook

In the nonunion system, the employee handbook serves as a structure for the governance of the workplace. It resembles the collective bargaining agreement, but it is not its equivalent. The handbook enables management to administer employee relations within the competitive framework and the law, and affords employees a written program outlining and defining their position within the company. The structure is supplemented by manuals on personnel policy and procedures. Management periodically reviews and updates these documents in the light of experience and legal developments. The handbook provides information about the company and the conditions of employment that employees expect and require. For these reason, employees do, in fact, regard the handbook as one of their most important sources of information, as survey information regularly indicates. It would be interesting for the sake of comparability to know how many workers in the organized system receive from the union representatives copies of their collective bargaining agreements and union constitutions, both of which affect their working lives, and just how important a source of information the agreements and constitutions are to them. Also, it would be useful to know how many union members are informed of their rights with respect to their union as provided by the Labor Management Reporting and Disclosure Act of 1959.

The details of the employee handbook personalize, or at least attempt to personalize, the relationship between the employee and the company. For example, handbooks, unlike collective bargaining agreements, provide employees with a chart of the company's line organization that enables the worker to locate his/her position in the establishment. Frequently, they also include a map of the installation as well. Handbooks often include a history of the company and its products. These details not only personalize the enterprise but give the individual a sense of belonging to an institution that is recognizable, significant, and useful to the community and the economy, and one that has a record of performance.

Illustrative of the scope of information handbooks provide employees about the company and its policies are as follows:

Introduction
Welcome to the company
Company history
Management philosophy
What to look for in your job
What is expected of you
Sexual harassment

Employee Patent and Confident-
  ial Information Agreement
Probationary employment
The supervisor and you
Complaint procedures
Communications
Disciplinary procedures
Prior employment service credit
Sexual harassment

Compensation Policies
Wages and job classes
Market survey
Job evaluation
Profit sharing
Performance appraisal
Salary increase
Shift premium
Meal allowance
Team norms
Sunday premium
Payday
Payroll deductions
Hours of work
Overtime
Time cards
Reporting and callback pay

Employee Policies and Practices
Employee rights
Code of conduct
Policy on equal employment
Layoff and recall policy
Seniority
Absenteeism and tardiness

Thrift and Stock Purchase Plan
Pension plan, including 401K plans
Payment for absence time
Jury duty
Bereavement pay
Short-term military pay
Holidays
Vacations
Educational assistance
Matching grants
Scholarships to children of
  employees/retirees
Suggestion system
Service awards

Safety and Health
Accident prevention and safety rules
Medical services
Eye protection
Footwear
Smoking and eating in the plant
Fire emergencies
Rest periods
Clean-up time
Sick/personal day policy
Leave of absence

Promotion Policy
Job postings
Seniority and merit
Performance appraisals

Benefits
Medical benefits
Dental assistance plan
Group insurance, life and
  accident
Disability programs
Travel accident plan

Miscellaneous
Telephone calls;
  bulletin boards
Parking
Personnel records
Dress code
Identification badge
No solicitation policy
Savings bonds; credit unions
Direct-deposit banking

Obviously, the document is fairly comprehensive. But how does the handbook compare with the collective bargaining agreement? It is often as detailed and comprehensive in covering employee relations as some bargaining agreements, but the differences between the two are far more significant than their similarities. The basic differences between them are in their intent, what they do, and their enforceability. The essence of the handbook is to facilitate management's function to manage, and yet to provide a framework for equitable and consistent treatment of the individual employee. Meantime, judicial interpretation and legislative enactments have made the document much more than a statement of good intent. In contrast, the essence of the collective bargaining agreement is to protect rights, the rights of the union as the bargaining representative, the rights of workers they represent, and those rights retained by management. The collective agreement focuses on the rights of adversarial parties, and these rights are legally enforceable, and that is its claim to superiority over the handbook.

To fulfill management philosophy of fair treatment, the handbook deals in detail with employees' jobs. The details include the wage structure and wage administration; the right to bring any problem in writing or verbally to their supervisor and to receive a timely answer; the right to appeal beyond the immediate supervisor; the right to be informed in writing personally or through the company bulletin board of all communications intended for general distribution; the right to be considered for any promotion or transfer opportunity that arises and for which the individual has the required skills and ability, before the vacancy is filled from outside; and the right to the full extent of benefits specified in the benefits package and to be free of unilateral decisions in conflict with policies and interpretations governing those benefits.

Managements treat those rights as legally unenforceable. However, growing legal limitations on employment at-will and interpretations by some courts have ruled that handbook promises are legally binding. For many years, courts, relying on standard contract law, ruled that because handbooks involved no "consideration," a legal term reflecting a reciprocal exchange of promises and/or things, these rights were not legally enforceable. Since the handbooks are unilateral documents, there was no consideration and hence no binding contract. Nevertheless, even in states that have limited employment at-will, there are rulings that distinguish the facts in specific cases from precedents, and therefore it is still accurate to say that most courts do not find that handbook promises are binding. At the same time, the challenges have led managements to include disclaimers intended to preserve management's right to amend, modify, or cancel the handbook; to deny any guarantee of continued employment and the right to terminate or lay off employees (Befort 1991/1992). Standard managerial policy continues to state that the reciprocity of responsibilities identified in the handbook does not constitute a contract, unless written agreements with individual employees have been approved by the company's board of directors. Handbooks typically disavow the authority of any official of the company to authorize an employment contract, or the assumption by any employee of any employment contract, written or oral. For example, one handbook states that "employment with [this company] and its subsidiaries is terminable at any time by the Employee or the Employer." When the employer discharges the employee, this handbook continues, "employment will not be terminated except for cause." Cause is defined to include "causes of any nature whatsoever including, but not limited to, business conditions, job eliminations, economic conditions and the performance and/or conduct of the employee."

Management provides a copy of the handbook to all employees, which they must sign. A member of management signs on behalf of the company. One major reason for the signing is to validate the legal disclaimer disavowing a legal contract of employment between the employer and the employee. An example of the disclaimer is the following:

> This handbook is neither an employment contract nor any other guarantee of full-time employment. An individual's continuous employment at [this company] is based upon such factors as customers needs, business conditions, corporate sales and profits, as well as an employee's skill and job performance.

The disclaimer is, of course, intended to protect the doctrine of employment at-will, and a leading critic of the at-will doctrine believes that the disclaimer passes legal muster: "Unequivocal language in a job application that any resulting employment will be only-at-will, or a clear and prominent disclaimer in an employee handbook that any policy statements are not legally binding, will generally foreclose employee claims" (St. PAntoine 1988, p. 61).

Nevertheless, the durability of employment at-will has been weakening for some time as a consequence of judicial interpretations. These interpretations are not only diluting the doctrine, but are finding their way into statutory enactments. In that way, employment law has begun to enhance workers' legal protection in the nonunion system of industrial relations, just as in the organized system. Hence it would be misleading to assume that employee rights to access the company's procedures, whether involving employment, the complaint system, promotions, wages and benefits, are without legal redress.

——————— Five ———————

Employee Communication

Supervisors

My study now turns from what makes the individual system possible and workers' and employers' preference for how it works. Essentially, the study shifts from a macro to a micro perspective of the individual system of representation in the next two chapters. In this chapter, I examine employee communication; in the next, how terms and conditions of employment are determined.

While I have stressed the importance of managerial commitment to the individual system as a policy commitment, carrying out this policy rests to a very large degree on the managerial person who interacts with the employees daily and on their most important concerns: the supervisor. The most important communications link between management and employees in the nonunion system, as in the organized system, is the supervisor. In fact, the supervisor is an even more significant link in the individual system because the supervisor's actions and treatment of subordinates can foster a favorable or unfavorable employee attitude toward nonunionism and therefore the success or failure of the system. Essentially, "the supervisor is the Company" to employees under the individual system. Because "the supervisor is the Company" to employees in the nonunion system, the supervisor is the management person who has most to do with the job and a worker's progress in his working career. The employee's closest contact is with the supervisor; the supervisor is the person to whom the employee reports, the one from whom he receives instructions, and to whom in the first instance he presents questions or complaints, and who disciplines or rewards him. In the organized system, the individual worker can turn to his union representative as an alternative, in part and on some issues, and whose presence curtails the authority of the supervisor.

The success of the supervisor in exercising his duties depends in no small part on the performance of those supervised. Thus, the supervisor has a direct reciprocal interest in the performance of the employees directly under his management. Their success or failure is also his. Therefore, from the perspective of the shop floor, the successful supervisor also represents the employees' interests to higher management. Conversely, the supervisor plays a key role in presenting management's philosophy and policies on individual representation. As one management official stated, "The major determinative factor in union elections and maintaining good employee relations [free of collective bargaining] is the relationship between employees and their supervisors." Unions have won representation elections where companies paid high wages and provided superior benefits, but also had poor relations between supervisors and employees; on the other hand, unions lost when supervision was doing its job. A study inimical to employers' efforts to ward off unions concluded that "opposition of supervisors was particularly effective in defeating union drives" (Freeman and Kleiner 1990, p. 351).

Because supervisors have the most contact with the individual worker, they are an essential communications link between the company's philosophy of individual representation and its application. Because of the supervisor's proximity to the employee, he implements and demonstrates management's concepts on all aspects of employee relations. To a large extent, employees' attitudes toward the company reflect their attitudes toward the supervisor. If the employee trusts, likes, and respects the supervisor, it is likely that those attitudes will be transferred to the employer. And that is why, to many workers, the supervisor is the company. Not surprisingly, therefore, numerous theoretical approaches to effective supervisory management have emerged from academic and management consultants, but to one practitioner "they are not panaceas; they are not quick fixes; they are not substitutes for good old-fashioned close relationships between supervisor and each employee." To paraphrase a well-known TV commercial, good supervision is acquired in the old-fashioned way: it has to be earned. How does nonunion management expect its supervisors to implement policy?

Management's assessment of the supervisory function begins with the recognition that the quality of supervisory leadership will necessarily vary. Although rigid and detailed rules are customarily avoided, management does establish guidelines for effective supervision especially attuned to nonunion employee relations. The guidelines consist of a number of "thou shall" and "thou shall not" precepts. The most important of the positive steps is that supervisors are called upon to focus on the individual worker, to know the individuals they supervise. On that principle, the supervisor is expected to respect those they supervise by recognizing that each is an individual and that the individual employee probably knows the details of the work better than anyone else. Such treatment makes it more likely for the individual worker to be forthcoming in making suggestions that can improve operations, from simplifying work processes to the substitution of new and different materials, and even changes that might make the final product more attractive to the consumer.

To make supervision function more efficiently, nonunion managements expect the employee to understand exactly what is expected of him and why, and to be held accountable, or rewarded as the case may be. Supervisors' ability to give clear instructions in the production process has a parallel in employee relations: if the supervisor knows and understands production, he should also know his business when explaining company policies and practices in employee relations. When employees perform well, another positive duty of supervisors is to recognize those achievements: "Pay an honest compliment for every good piece of work you see, and make it a point to watch for good work." Credit for achievement is a recurring expectation in survey results of employee attitudes.

Supervisors are expected to get employees involved in resolving problems of the company, to be available to answer questions, and to hear and listen to complaints. It has been argued that employees' participation in problem solving can be durable only if the process is diffused over large numbers of workers and is reinforced by policies such as employment security (Kochan, Katz and McKersie 1986, pp. 87–88). In the nonunion system, the extent of diffusion depends on the supervisors; in the union system, the diffusion must be screened through the shop steward. Nonunion managements regard this as an impediment to harmonious employee relations and an example of what they mean by "third party" interference.

Supervisors are expected to handle questions and grievances effectively. If they do not or cannot, supervisors become the first step in the more formal complaint procedure. The other side of the complaint procedure in the nonunion system is its potential for trivialization of issues. One nonunion manager of employee relations explained the issue this way:

> If you have a meeting every time someone claims there is too much sugar on the doughnuts, your employees will not only conclude that you like meetings, they will make sure you have plenty of them. If you stroke stupidity, you get more of it. When you get enough stupidity and stop stroking, people find it hard to understand why you stopped having meetings to talk about petty gripes.

Discipline is the responsibility of the supervisor, and he is expected to exercise it in the nonunion system no less than in the union system. Whether disciplinary action takes the form of a correction, reprimand, warning, or discharge, the goal is the improvement of the worker's performance, and not necessarily the punishment. However, supervisors' effectiveness is subverted when higher management limits or forbids suspension, a practice that may happen because of higher management's apprehension that the strict application of employment policies will bring on the union.

Foremost of the "thou shall not" directives is playing favorites. This issue and its "flip side," fairness, are standard issues raised by employees in attitude surveys, and negative findings are treated as "red alerts" by higher management, often leading to training for supervisors. Another remedy is the "open door" policy, which enables a disgruntled employee to go to higher management when he feels wronged by the supervisor. This avenue is also part of the complaint procedure, reviewed later in this chapter. The "open door" has pitfalls for both management and the individual employee. If it leads to undercutting the supervisor, it weakens plant discipline. At the same time, the complaining employee may later find himself subject to subtle discrimination by the supervisor. Nevertheless, the Harris study for the AFL-CIO in 1984 found frequent recourse to supervisors and higher management by individuals as well as by groups in the nonunion setting.

Because of their strategic position in the chain of management, nonunion management makes considerable investment in the training of their supervisors. Supervisory training is mainly in-house, but is also supplemented in some companies by seminars, professional management programs, and short courses given by trade associations or local colleges. Because communications between the worker and human resource management typically begin with the supervisor, supervisors are trained in human relations. Company policies are explained and reviewed regularly to enable supervisors to interpret those policies to the individual employee in understandable language. Supervisors are encouraged to develop and maintain strong individual relationships with employees. As one management stated it: ". . . the real heart of our effort must be regular, ongoing, face-to-face, one-on-one communications between supervisors and their employees."

The supervisor's training is intended to teach him to listen to employees. Higher managements in many instances criticize supervisors for giving short shrift to employee queries, although they add that they recognize the pressures supervisors may be under on occasion. The supervisor's guideline on "good listening" is not to interrupt an employee's statement, to avoid instant answers, and, in fact, to ask questions if necessary to understand what the worker is saying. The supervisor is expected to regard complaints as an opportunity to clear up a problem, or perhaps a management policy that has been misdirected, or to correct a managerial error, and not to be regarded as a time-consuming burden. The guidelines caution supervisors not to ridicule complaints, even if they are in fact petty, because the employee's perspective must also be understood. The supervisor is encouraged to resolve issues, if possible. Higher managements require supervisors to conduct periodic meetings with employees, to keep abreast of shop-floor issues. These shop meetings may be scheduled during or outside regular working hours. In the latter case, employees are paid for the time involved. Scheduling is arranged to enable all to participate at one time or another. Attendance is theoretically voluntary, but there is an expectation that employees as well as management representatives will attend. The agenda is elastic with the goal of addressing issues of current mutual interest.

What do supervisors tell employees? What do the employees want to know? Is there a match between the two? Or, are they complements? Survey results suggest that supervisors' and employees' agenda complement each other. According to the survey data, the supervisors' agenda tends to emphasize issues affecting basic business conditions, such as the status of customer orders, additions and replacement of facilities, and changes in the organizational structure of the company. Supervisors' agenda also includes information affecting employees' wages, job security, and promotion. Workers also want most to know about the company's future plans and about such matters as personnel policies and practices, productivity, job related information, and job advancement opportunities; they also want appreciation for their work, a feeling of being involved and getting sympathetic help on personal problems. These employee interests are the human resource functions expected of supervisors. The supervisor in his role as a human resource manager is instrumental in getting employees involved in solving problems and making improvements in the business. The theory behind this goal is that "when people feel they are not members of an organization, they tend to defeat it" (Myers 1976, p. 82). A variety of techniques are employed in getting employees involved in problem solving. Some are aimed at the individual, others at a group.

Another key responsibility of supervisors is to maintain open and frequent communication with their employees in both "upward and downward" directions. This was one of the ingredients of the production and human resource process at the nonunion

Nissan plant in Smyrna, Tennessee, as illustrated by the comments of a supervisor promoted to that position from the assembly line: "Everywhere I've worked before this, the way we worked pretty much came down as a directive. It's always better if we ask the people who are doing the job and don't dictate to them" (Levin 1989, p. 8). "Upward and downward" communications are intended to minimize the "we–they" atmosphere in the collective bargaining model: "By keeping workers closely informed about model changes, business trends and company news, Nissan managers aimed to instill a sense that the destinies of all employees were linked, an ideological notion opposite that of the orthodox U.A.W. line" (Levin 1989, p. 8). The communications system at Nissan doubtless contributed to the defeat of the United Auto Workers-AFL-CIO in a representation election by a 2–1 vote.

Communication between the supervisor and the employee is the most important process capable of preventing the escalation of gripes into complaints. This requires the supervisor to be out on the floor, readily available, easily approachable, ready to listen, able to understand the employees' viewpoint and to respond knowledgeably. This is intended to keep supervisors from spending too much time in the office, distancing themselves from workers, and making it difficult for employees to approach them. Getting management out of the office is essential to communication effectiveness. Moving from the office to the floor demonstrates supervisory accessibility in communications and management's interest in employees and their working conditions. This prescription is followed by higher management in smaller companies; they call it "managing by walking around."

A measure of the significance of supervisors in the communications link between management and employees is employees' ranking of supervisors as the primary source from which they most preferred to gain information, according to company survey data. After supervisors, employees' other preferred sources of information were small-group meetings with top management. These results not only show that workers clearly preferred gaining information about the company from face-to-face communications but give additional credence to the individual capable of acting on his own behalf in the individual system of industrial relations. Grape-vine information ranks only second in importance to supervisors as a source of information to workers. Does this suggest that some of the institutional channels of communication were not functioning so well? It might, but despite human resource management's efforts to make periodic meetings of employees with plant manager, and de-partment supervisors (and human resource staff), a regular, orga-nized source of information, reliance on the grapevine can never be displaced even by the most orderly arrangements; it is too ingrained in human behavior and characterizes the organized plant as well. Significantly, the company handbook ranked third as an actual source and fourth in preference, a finding that highlights its importance and relevance in the individual system of industrial relations.

Other Channels of Communication

For new employees in many nonunion settings, communication begins with orientation meetings with the employment relations manager, the supervisor, and general manager. It continues with weekly departmental meetings and regular monthly meetings with the plant manager or supervisor, usually conducted in a "town hall" manner. Perhaps "focus groups" in political life approximate these meetings. Plant meetings are more frequent under the individual than the union system (Verma 1983, p. 130). Topics are wide rang-ing, depending on circumstances, but often include the company's financial condition. Higher managements attend periodically to discuss previously announced topics and to respond to questions. In some companies, there are meetings and discussions with cor-porate-level employee relations management and randomly cho-sen employees. Periodic luncheon meetings with line or employee relations managers, or "coffee with the boss" sessions, add to the face-to-face approach, the most effective medium of communica-tions, according to survey information.

Another personal method is the use of short briefings between supervisors and department heads and employees. At these meet-ings, the agenda is usually limited to recent events and what is expected in the near future. Because of their limited agenda, briefings enable the individual employee to contribute to the discussion and for the supervisor or department head to gather data for better decisions. Company events and outings also offer managerial access to family members. These are regarded as highly important to the nonunion company because they afford an opportunity for management to meet employees and their families on a social and personal level, strengthening loyalty to the company. Such sessions are intended not only to present information but also to build the company's image of an employer interested in the individual employee and the local community.

Probably next in value after a personal meeting is television. It can present issues in a personalized context. Overuse and trivialization, however, undermine credibility. Print media are also used in the communications system. Newsletters are passed out at the job site and are mailed. The contents address accomplishments of the company or its division in introducing new products, the integration of newly acquired companies, the movement of units to other locations, and personal information about employees. Company magazines as well as newsletters are used by the larger employers, newsletters by the smaller ones. Mailing offers another opportunity to communicate directly with the employee and his family. Some nonunion employers provide their employees with an annual financial report of the company. It reports trends in sales, profits, profit margins, capital spending, the cost of benefits (total and per employee), and medical care. Employees view these data in terms of their work for the company, or at least that is management's hope.

Surveys of employee attitudes are viewed as the "bottom up" approach in communications. This method is formal and systematic and is intended to supply management with detailed information about employee attitudes and lead to corrective actions. Comparisons over time within the company and with national benchmarks are expected to answer former New York Mayor Ed Koch's question, "How am I doing?" Managements contend that they give serious attention to the findings of surveys, just as politicians do to political polls. The questions are oriented to elicit employee assessments of the employment relationship and how well the enterprise is performing: (1) Is the company a good place to work? (2) Is management running things well, and are managers interested in the employees? (3) Does the supervisor run things well, treat me like a human, listen, or play favorites? (4) On pay and benefits, how do they compare with other companies, and is the information adequate on benefits? (5) Is there employment security? (6) Do you feel free to speak up? (7) Are reductions in force handled fairly? (8) On promotions, were job openings made known to all, and did you receive fair consideration? (9) Are you satisfied with the training and development programs? (10) Were the objectives of the company and department explained, and was your work well planned? (11) Is the company's effort to inform adequate? (12) Were the company's rules applied consistently, and are you satisfied with the actions taken on grievances and complaints? (13) Did you receive recognition for good work? (14) In terms of personal satisfaction, were you treated well, is the work interesting and challenging, how is the morale of co-workers, and do you believe the employees and management are committed to the success of the company? (15) With reference to the physical conditions of employment, how do you rate the cafeteria, vending machines, housekeeping, lighting, heating, air conditioning, and ventilation of your working environment? Given the scope of the employee survey, management hopes to keep its hand on the "pulse" of employees. It is very detailed and searches for the quality of the basic connections between management and employees. Neither the survey nor the entire system of communications is a guarantor of nonunionism. Unorganized workers, as management is often reminded, still choose unions, albeit at a diminishing rate.

Complaint Systems

Fundamental to any relationship in labor relations is a means for employees to raise issues and to voice complaints, irrespective of whether the setting is nonunion or organized; a complaint system is, as one analyst wrote, "an enduring feature of industrial relations systems" (Lewin et al. 1997, p. 197). For the individual system, a credible complaint system is one of its basic elements:

> . . . the nonunion employer understandably is inclined to view the grievance procedure as a must in its program to remain nonunion [because] it has . . . been convincingly demonstrated that the success of unionization is a fairly direct function of the failure of management to discover and attend to employees' dissatisfaction. (Epstein 1975, p. 7)

The complaint procedures may be formal or informal; how prevalent they are in the individual system is unknown, but my impression is that they are used on a substantial scale. Irrespective of type, most complaints are resolved informally (Lewin et al. 1997, pp. 197–198). Resort to the complaint procedure is not only implicit in the market rationale for the individual system of representation, but it has been explicitly recognized in the basic law of labor relations, the National Labor Relations Act, as amended, 1947. Section 9 (a) of the amended act, the Taft-Hartley Act, specifically provides that

> . . . any individual employee or a group of employees shall have a right at any time to present grievances to their employer and to have such grievances adjusted, without the intervention of the bargaining representative.

Although this language refers to the organized system of representation, it is applicable to the nonunion system as well; the First Amendment to the Constitution also assures that right. Changes in the National Labor Relations Act have doubtless been responsible for the sharp increase in the number of nonunion complaint systems since the end of World War II.

The nonunion complaint systems serve two functions. One is to discover and attend to employee dissatisfactions and to remedy complaints, in other words, to do what any complaint system should do. They demonstrate to the employees that the system fulfills the purpose of the audits of employee concerns and the employee handbook. Second, the complaint system contributes significantly to the ability of the company to remain nonunion. The complaint system addresses any complaint about any alleged unfair treatment. It can arise under the handbook, past practice, or anything arising out of the work relationship. This gives the nonunion grievance system greater flexibility than the organized system because it can address any problem. In contrast, the grievance procedures under collective bargaining must link the grievance to a specific term of the collective bargaining agreement or to established practice. The principal weakness of the nonunion system is that it can lead to the trivialization of issues, as noted above. The organized system suffers from a parallel shortcoming, that of forcing meritless complaints through the grievance procedure in order for the union to show that it is ready to represent its members vigorously. If the nonunion system's major shortcoming is the potential for trivialization, the organized system's fault is to convert any alleged violation into a political stance. Moreover, the organized systems' reference point, workers' rights under the agreement and past practice, tends to make the grievance procedure legalistic and rigid.

Conductors of a study of a small number of nonunion businesses done at Columbia University from 1985 to 1988 were surprised to find that between 42 percent and 54 percent had written grievance procedures for one or another employee group (Lewin 1990). They were also surprised to discover that about one of every five included third-party arbitration. Likewise, results from another study showed limited use of arbitration (McCabe 1988). In 1995, the Boeing Company instituted an alternative dispute resolution process for the firm's approximately 100,000 nonunion workers that provided for binding arbitration opportunities for workplace disputes that cannot be settled by the employee and his supervisor. Despite the size and importance of Boeing, the arbitration step is unlikely to establish a precedent for nonunion companies generally because it was doubtless instituted for internal employee relations. Boeing's production and engineering workforces are highly unionized, and their contracts include arbitration as part of the grievance procedure, so it is likely that the institution of arbitration for the company's nonunion workers was intended to give them similar arrangements without the need for union representation. In general, nonunion managements avoid arbitration because of their wariness of transferring decision making to an outsider, who not only may be unfamiliar with the company's culture and operations, but, most compelling, is in itself a contradiction of the fundamental principle of the individual system, a third party in the labor relationship.

Do nonunion workers exercise their right to present complaints to their employers? The Columbia data reported that the average rate is approximately 40 percent lower than that of unionized businesses, but the Harris study indicated that nonunion workers resorted to their companies' complaint system on a far greater scale. Almost 70 percent of nonunion employees surveyed in the Harris report went to their employers as individuals to resolve work-related issues, and of these, more than 80 percent asserted that they were satisfied or very satisfied with the response. In addition, more than one-quarter of nonunion workers went to their employer as a group over work-related matters. Of these, more than three-fourths said they were satisfied or very satisfied by the outcome (Harris and Associates 1984, Table 17, p. 60). Moreover, nearly 60 percent of nonunion workers said that their employer willingly dealt with workplace problems (Harris and Associates 1984, Table 18, p. 41). Perhaps even more surprising is the fact that Harris found that more than 60 percent of union members went to their employers on their own to resolve work-related problems (Harris and Associates 1984, Table 17, p. 60). Clearly, Taft-Hartley's revisions allowing individual union members to present their own grievances had filtered through to workers, organized and unorganized. Nevertheless, it is unlikely that management in organized relations would deal fully with complaints presented by individual union members, as would nonunion management, because of its reluctance to antagonize the union representing their employees. On the same issue, a Penn and Schoen survey of May 1993 found that even 73 percent of union members said that employees would rather speak for themselves, and 69 percent of the public at large agreed. Evidently, individual representation even survives under collective bargaining. Such findings are support for the finding that nonunion complaint systems address the individual worker's grievances.

Most grievances in the nonunion setting are settled at the lower levels of the procedures. Lewin reported that only about one of every 500 grievances initially filed reached the last step of the procedure. Where arbitration was part of the procedure, however, resort to the final step was more frequent, reflecting the individual's desire to reach the company's "Supreme Court" in hopes of eventual vindication. The most common issues found by the Columbia study among nonunion companies generally coincided with the unionized businesses, indicating that work experience is much the same irrespective of the form of representation. How these problems are resolved is different, as might be expected. The Columbia data also found that appeals to higher management did, on occasion, reverse lower-level managerial decisions. The practice has two conflicting possible outcomes: it validates the nonunion system in the judgment of the employees, but it also tends to undercut the authority of supervisors and other lower management, an infirmity in the procedures noted above.

Critics of the nonunion complaint system (Ewing 1977, 1989) contend that it cannot truly resolve complaints because it lacks an adversary to the employer (the union) to represent the employee; or that it lacks (or most do lack) an outside arbitrator, one who could render an impartial decision; and that the complaint system is rarely used. Yet, both the Columbia and Harris findings contradict the criticism of the nonunion complaint system on the grounds that the individual cannot, or will not, represent himself. Indeed, the Harris study reported that the willingness to present grievances was found among all occupational, demographic, and income groups in the nonunion system. While professional and sales groups led with 72 percent saying they went on their own to the employer about work-related problems, majorities of service and unskilled workers, the skilled, and all other white-collar occupations also went on their own. Men and women were evenly divided in their usage of the procedures, 69 percent of each group representing themselves. By age category, three-quarters of those in the 35–44 age group presented their own grievances. Most complaints, Harris found, had to do with personal problems; job dissatisfaction was not responsible for the extensive use of the complaint system. In fact, Harris found nonunion employees overwhelmingly satisfied with their job, and this led Harris to conclude that the nonunion worker regarded union representation as irrelevant to this job.

McCabe's study reports that more nonunion systems are moving toward internal arbitration. McCabe favors outside arbitration, as a feature that he believes would add to the credibility of the nonunion complaint system. However, most managements in the nonunion domain reject outside arbitrators for reasons already given: wariness of transferring decision making to an outsider, who may be unfamiliar with the company's culture and operations, and because arbitration contradicts the fundamental reasons of the individual system, including a third party in the labor relationship.

Three basic types of internal review systems have emerged in the nonunion system (McCabe 1988). These are "open-door" with formal appeal; peer review with internal arbitration; and third, internal review with external arbitration. All share a common goal and a common problem. The goal of the nonunion systems, as in the organized system, is fairness in resolving any problems that an employee has with the company, supervisor, or any aspect of the job. In turn, it also seeks to resolve any problems that the company has with employees. But can the nonunion system afford due process to workers in the resolution of their grievances? To analyze the issue of due process, I begin with McCabe's definition of a complaint in the nonunion system as "an employee's expressed feeling of dissatisfaction concerning conditions of employment or treatment by management or other employees" (McCabe 1988, p. 124). The open door system (with formal appeal) allows an individual to approach a management official to discuss his problem, and so "employees can talk to anyone at anytime about anything" (McCabe, 1988, p. 121). This informal route, the "open door," is separate from formal grievance procedures. It can and does deal with complaints, but it is also an avenue for general communications with employees. As noted above, some companies require higher management, including chief operating officers, to spend time at the plant, to be seen, and to be accessible to employees periodically: "Two or three times a year, the president of the company and his staff meet with all the employees to communicate what is going on in the company." In another, "The corporate CEO visits each location twice a year, and usually holds one large rally where they review the local business and may respond to questions from the employees." This visibility is intended to give credence to the open-door complaint procedure.

Under the formal procedure, the grievant follows a series of steps, ranked in ascending order of managerial authority:

1. The first step is for the grievant to discuss the problem with the immediate supervisor. The supervisor will then respond promptly with a verbal answer. (This step will be waived if circumstances dictate.)

2. If not satisfied with the answer, the grievant may request that the supervisor arrange a meeting with the plant superintendent. At this step, all parties involved will be given an opportunity to meet and discuss the issues. Within a time specified, usually in the handbook (five working days, for example), the grievant will receive a written answer with copies to all individuals who had attended the meeting.

3. The grievant, if dissatisfied, can proceed to the next step. In this, the final step, the grievant can meet with the top management of the company or plant. Within a specified time, that official will render a written answer, which will be final and binding on all parties.

McCabe, who has done a detailed analysis of these systems, commented that he was surprised at the number of companies that had an open door coupled with a formal system of successive hierarchical steps of appeal that could overrule lower ranks of management. The large number of appeal steps reflects a desire for due process. McCabe concluded that the open-door system, the most popular among nonunion companies, is central to nonunion managements' philosophy and is "the keystone of sound management relations [with employees]" (McCabe 1988, p. 161). Nonunion managements share this view: "We try very hard to settle differences at the lowest level possible and urge all our employees to use our open door policy."

The second complaint system increasingly coming into use in nonunion employee relations is a review with internal arbitration (McCabe 1988). This system provides internal binding arbitration by a panel of employees, some with and some without members from management. The procedure consists of steps similar to those in the open-door system, but it substitutes the final judgment of the panel for that of a company official. The peer-review panel may consist of an odd or even number of members. If even numbered, the otherwise nonvoting chair votes in a tie. The chair may be selected by the grievant from the personnel department. All panel members may come from the employees or management or consist of a majority drawn from the employees and the balance from management (three employees, two management, for example). Employee representatives are chosen from a pool of volunteers who have taken training in complaint procedures and have a minimum service with the company; each serves for a period of one year. The grievant chooses both the employee and employer representatives on the review panel. In some, however, the industrial relations manager is a permanent member, and the divisional manager appoints the other management panel member.

The complainant may present his own case or have another person from within the company represent him before the panel. (The panel takes jurisdiction within a specified time following the rejection of the grievance in the preceding step, normally by the supervisor or plant manager.) The grievant, or his representative, may call any witnesses and obtain all data germane to the case from the employer. The supervisor or other management official representing the company may do likewise. In some instances, the panel investigates the grievance as well as interrogates presenters and witnesses. A majority renders a decision binding on the parties. Usually, it must be issued within five working days of the hearing. If it is determined that the grievant is owed back pay, the panel may so order, less any interim compensation. In some cases, higher management may choose between a managerial decision and panel arbitration. The internal tribunal is limited to the issues before it, but its decision cannot change company policy.

McCabe found that there is no underlying principle governing the internal tribunal system among the twenty-six of seventy-eight companies he studied. His conclusion was based on the fact that only one-third had installed the internal tribunal procedure, and that in only one company did he find an acknowledgment in the handbook that the employee had a right to be heard (McCabe 1988, pp. 111–112). Further, the term "peer review," used by companies that have an internal tribunal, cannot be fairly described as such because some panels include management participation.

The third type of complaint system is arbitration by an outside professional, just as in the unionized system. This is the least widespread of the three nonunion complaint systems. McCabe found only six among the seventy-eight companies he studied. Methods of selecting the arbitrator varied from employee selection, management selection, joint selection, and designation by the American Arbitration Association. The arbitrator is paid by the company, except in one instance where the employee pays a small fee if he loses. The scope of the arbitration award is circumscribed: ". . . the arbitrator's assigned function is to determine whether the employee or management violated a published rule of the company, and he may not consider whether the rule [itself] is unfair or unreasonable" (McCabe 1988, pp. 76–77). This proviso is intended to keep policymaking in the hands of management and avoid its dilution by arbitrators. Nonunion managements regard this as insulation from the doctrine that the decisions of arbitrators are legally enforceable. It should be noted that the Columbia study found that nonunion systems paid employees for time dedicated to the implementation of the grievance procedures.

In his assessment of the nonunion complaint system, McCabe favors arbitration, either internal or external, and sees a constructive role for an ombudsman and outside mediation (McCabe 1988, pp. 174–179). However, most nonunion management typically regards participation by an outside party to decide disputes as tantamount to conceding that it cannot really manage without a third party. That procedure, they argue, would reject the basic tenet of the system of individual representation. If a third party, an arbitrator, is needed to resolve internal differences, why should not employees come to believe that another third party—a union—is needed to resolve all issues between them and management? For the same reason that nonunion managements object to arbitration, they also reject the use of an ombudsman and of mediation. To them, an ombudsman is arbitration by the back door; mediation requires an outside (third) party and is rejected for the same reason.

Nonunion management's preferred system, the open door, has important deficiencies. Primarily, it has a propensity to undercut supervisory and other levels of managerial authority. If these groups are overruled frequently, their authority is undermined and can weaken what supervisors and lower managements are hired to do— make decisions.

> We do not subscribe to the theory that if the employee perceives a problem, it must be a problem. Such employees must change their attitude. If they can't, they tend to go away on a Friday afternoon. No one misses them. Likewise, peer pressure in our shop causes constant complainers to lose face.

The open door may also contribute to shirking rather than productive shmoozing, but in the nonunion setting, the more flexible work arrangements forestall reduction of productivity. Hamermesh (1988) defined shmoozing in the workplace as time spent socializing with co-workers, which contributes to productivity and higher wages; shirking has the opposite effects. Both union and nonunion workers are found to shirk, but shirking is apparently more extensive among nonunion workers (Hamermesh 1988, pp. 2, 13, 14). This suggests that supervision and discipline are not as tight in nonunion shops as higher management apparently believes.

Can the nonunion system meet its principles of a fair dealing and due process? It can and does, but like its counterpart in the organized system, it is imperfect. Critics contend that due process is inherently absent in the nonunion system because of the absence of the third party, the union and the arbitrator. While due process is ultimately a matter for the courts and employment law to resolve, there is also an economic dimension to fair dealing. Human capital theory emphasizes the necessity of conserving the investment in the worker, an investment made by the employer and the individual. Rational behavior, the premise underlying economic action in a competitive society, encourages an economic or industrial relations due process in the workplace. If the system, individual or organized, fails to provide due process, whether economic or in matters of civil rights, the employees themselves have procedures to rectify the wrong: a representation election to choose a union, or a decertification election to rid themselves of an unfair organized representation. Meantime, the fact is that nonunion employees do exercise their right to present complaints and are generally satisfied by the results, according to surveys and the prevalence of the individual system in the labor market.

Disciplinary Procedures

While the focus so far has been on the employees' problems with management, employers also have problems with employees in the nonunion system. Just as the individual has expectations of the company, the company has reciprocal expectations of the employee, in particular with respect to job performance and working within the established work rules on safety and regular and on-time attendance. In the representative nonunion company, complaints over an employee's behavior begin with the identification of the problem. Typically, this is followed by a counseling session with the supervisor. The supervisor will advise the employee of the problem, discuss what needs to be done to correct the problem, and agree on a time period for correcting it. Should the issue persist, a second counseling session with the supervisor is scheduled, followed by formal notification of the specific steps the employee must take to bring his performance to a satisfactory level. A memorandum detailing this record is put into the individual's personnel file. The final step would be dismissal, based on cause.

When dismissal is called for, management can often rely on the approbation of the worker's fellow employees "because our work environment is so intense that when a worker is continually not pulling his weight, the other employees feel put out. They want the employee dealt with." In effect, employees expect management to manage, a surprising judgment. This attitude especially may be the case where profit sharing is a part of the compensation program. Employees do not approve of the notion that "discipline is nonpunitive in our company." If nonunion management errs in its labor relations, it has probably erred most on the issue of discipline. Legally, dismissal under the contemporary handbook is increasingly challenged by the courts. While the employees' handbook disavows any employment contract, explicitly or implicitly, courts have, at times, treated the handbook as creating a contract, limiting the doctrine of employment at-will. However, since all violations are not those listed in the handbook, the authority to fire remains unrestricted to a large extent.

Disciplinary procedures vary by company, and by type of employee and occupation. Broadly, blue-collar disciplinary procedures are more formal and closer to those in the unionized system of industrial relations. The more formal disciplinary procedure classifies violations of rules into several categories. The lowest level are those violations that are nuisances, but that, if uncorrected, may develop into major problems. These are failure to attend required meetings, stopping work before schedule, loitering, creating or contributing to unsanitary conditions, neglect of or mishandling equipment, waste or personal use of company property, and unsatisfactory work and attitude. Disciplinary steps for such offenses escalate from a written warning for the first offense, a written warning for the second, followed by a meeting with the supervisor for counseling and the employee's commitment to correct the violation, and finally, after the fourth offense, termination of employment.

The second category of violations, though serious, may have extenuating circumstances permitting a more lenient treatment. These violations consist of leaving the assigned working area during working hours without permission of the supervisor, use of profanity or vulgarity, violation of the no-solicitation or distribution rules, abuse of break or lunch privileges, and absence without leave. The disciplinary steps are the same as in the first category, except the number of steps is reduced. The third categories of violations are more serious and are therefore subject to immediate suspension pending discharge. These are fighting, assault, bribery, gambling, or criminal acts, reporting to work with detectable traces of alcoholic beverages or controlled substances, insubordination, disorderly conduct, or other acts detrimental to the welfare of the company. One offense can lead to termination of employment.

Written warnings are completely written-off six months after issuance if there is no other disciplinary penalty. Final warnings require twelve months to wipe out, subject to the absence of any additional disciplinary actions. All notices must be signed by the employee. This is not understood to mean acceptance by the employee of the warning, but that he has been notified. Most disciplinary policies among nonunion employers are not as formal and are more lenient than the foregoing language would imply. For example, while regular attendance and punctuality are expected and taken into consideration in job performance, pay increases, and promotion, the disciplinary procedure assumes that the workers understand their responsibilities:

> If there is excessive absence or lateness, or if a pattern of absence is observed, it will first be called to your attention privately by your supervisor. . . . If, after discussion with your supervisor, the situation persists, your supervisor will consult with the Personnel Department and disciplinary action, which can result in separation, may be initiated.

Discipline is certainly enforced under the individual system of representation, but it is neither as harsh nor as uncompromising as the language of the foregoing procedures suggests. The reported attitudes of employees in surveys indicate that on the whole nonunion workers are satisfied with the results. The preponderance of the individual system in the labor market attests to that attitude in the workplace. If that were not the case, the union option is always available. However, nonunion workers have turned to that option in diminishing numbers, as secret ballot elections conducted by the NLRB demonstrate (Chapter 8).

———— Six ————

Conditions of Employment

Compensation

Quality wages and benefits are key building blocks in both systems of industrial relations. For the nonunion system, quality conditions of employment play no less a role in attaching workers to individual representation than collectively bargained conditions attach union workers to unionism. However, the most important fact about the terms of employment in the nonunion model is to understand a negative: what they do not do. Contrary to the conventional wisdom, the nonunion system does not gain or secure individual representation by buying it. Paying compensation above the market will not keep the union out; paying below the market will ease its arrival, but will not guarantee it.

Some nonunion employers are leaders in employment conditions because, like some unionized employers, they occupy special positions in the markets they sell and therefore are able to compensate employees at above what would be competitive levels. This policy, the policy of high wages, is economically rational because it assists employers to recruit, train, and retain quality workers whose productivity offsets higher costs, enabling the company to compete. Competition, as already emphasized, is based on unit costs of production. For example, one nonunion ministeel producer asserted that because of its high productivity, it is the lowest-cost producer of its product in the world, exemplifying that unit labor costs, not wage rates by themselves, determine the ability to compete.

Although a high wage policy may characterize a company, nonunion and union, a particular employer may not be able to use this policy. For that employer, the compensation policy on wages and benefits is to keep abreast of the market. For that employer, local labor markets determine the conditions of employment, both for the internal wage structure and across competitive firms. Generally, those employers surveyed asserted that "employees have a right to expect their wages to be earned in accordance with their ability and skills, and their contribution to the productive output of [the company]." In turn, "[the company] has a responsibility to pay wages and provide benefits which are equitable and competitive within its industry and community in which it operates." No doubt these are some self-serving statements, but that is no more reason to question their validity than it would be to question the union slogan of a "fair day's pay for a fair day's work." In economic terms, the nonunion management expression just quoted encapsulates the marginal productivity theory of wages.

Empirically, nonunion management focuses on "wages and benefits being competitive in the local labor market rather than matching union or overall industry levels" (Verma 1983, p. 169). This flexibility in wage policy gives the representative nonunion firm a competitive advantage over its unionized rivals, which seek to "nationalize" wage standards, that is, to "take wages out of competition." The confrontation in 1989 between the nonunion Nissan management at the company's factory in Tennessee and the United Auto Workers (UAW) illustrates the role of wages in relation to other aspects of the conditions of employment in the nonunion setting: Even though the "average Nissan wage of more than $11 does not match the UAW wage rate . . . it is competitive" (Levin 1989, p. 8). Despite their knowledge of the higher union scale, Nissan workers rejected by 2 to 1 the opportunity to join the UAW in a National Labor Relations Board (NLRB) representation election.

Clearly, an individual worker weighs other factors in evaluating the benefits and costs of collective versus individual representation. As important as are wages, job security and job satisfaction also constitute values on which workers decide on representation.

To many nonunion workers, many of whom are former union members, the inability of unions to provide employment security weakens the attractiveness of organized representation. In fact, to many nonunion workers, unionism has become synonymous with employment insecurity. Many workers, nonunion and union, and the public confuse the term job security with employment security. Job security protects workers from arbitrary employer discharge by collective bargaining agreements and by legal limitations, but it has little to do with security of employment. Nonunion workers understand the difference and act on it.

Wage-rate studies of comparable nonunion and unionized workers have shown that unionized workers have a relative advantage (Lewis 1986). However, the analyses on which these findings are based may not capture important elements of employers' demand for labor, so that some of the relative advantage of unionized workers may be attributed to factors other than collective bargaining. Thus, a unionized firm that practiced a high-wage policy prior to unionization would continue to do so, only now with the additional pressure for higher wages coming from collective bargaining. Such a firm was in a position to pay higher wages and benefits out of earnings before and after unionization because it generated profits from a market that economists identify as imperfectly competitive. In effect, the employer shared monopoly profits with its employees (Hirsch 1991). Unions add to the existing compensation advantage of firms in concentrated industries: " . . . we would conclude that our estimates . . . indicate considerable redistribution from capital to unionized labor . . . where . . . unionism is positively correlated with concentration" (Voos and Mishel 1986, pp. 106, 129).

Still, other factors account for the differential between comparable union and nonunion workers. One such is compensating differentials. Compensating differentials are wage premiums paid for unpleasant and/or dangerous aspects of the job, a concept that Adam Smith introduced more than 200 years ago. Contemporary economists, in applying it to analyze the union/nonunion differential, have indeed found that Smith's concept does contribute to the higher wages of unionized workers (Duncan and Stafford 1980). An extension of this analysis has concluded that while a pure union differential exists, significant parts of unions' wage advantage may be attributable to compensating differentials—the unpleasant aspects of jobs and employment risk in the organized sector (Heywood 1989). Among the unpleasant aspects of jobs associated with unionized workplaces are rigid job structures, which define each job's responsibilities. Paradoxically, when unionized workers shirk (take unscheduled breaks), the shirking has been found to raise their productivity because it gives them a rest from the tedium and rigor of structured job requirements (Hamermesh 1988, pp. 2, 13, 14). The job requirements, in great measure a product of collective bargaining, reduce productivity. Shirking therefore introduces a degree of flexibility to the job. Again, Adam Smith anticipated this association between rigid job structures and productivity. He pointed out that the repetitiveness of the job increases the tedium of labor and diminishes workers' productivity. Thus, shirking is an act of "mutiny" against the rigors of collectively bargained job descriptions.

By contrast, shirking by nonunion workers has a negative effect on productivity. Shirking by nonunion workers does what one expects from goofing off: it lowers productivity. The reason is that shirking in the more open work structure of nonunion jobs detracts from working time and therefore performance. Shirking in the nonunion setting adds additional on-the-job leisure by nonunion workers. However, the more flexible work arrangements under the individual system of representation surmount this negative effect, and in the end nonunion firms are more productive and efficient than comparable union companies, as demonstrated by statistical studies (Hirsch 1991; Long, 1993).

In contrast to wage-rate comparisons, which are typically at a point in time, like a snapshot, a study of the effect of the unionization of manufacturing establishments (plants) spanning about three decades of data, 1963 to 1989, found "no evidence that a union's certification affects employees' annual or hourly wages either in the short or the long term [and that] this result holds for both small and large manufacturing plants (LaLonde, Marschke, and Troske 1996, p. 178). The authors speculated that the threat of unionization may have induced nonunion management to raise wages in the face of being organized and that this may have accounted for the

absence of a union wage advantage. An objection to that speculation is that when unions win, they insist on a wage increase in
order to validate their success, and this would have shown up in
their results. The authors concluded that unionization imposes "substantial nonpecuniary costs on the plant." They also found "substantial declines in production worker employment, hours,
shipments and material costs [and that these] persist for at least
nine years following the year of the [representation] election and
appear to affect the company not just the plant" (LaLonde,
Marschke, and Troske 1996, pp. 177–178.). In contrast to nearly
all statistical studies comparing union-nonunion wages, this study's
unit of observation was plant and was extended over many years;
the conventional method's study uses comparable individual workers and is for a point in time, whether annual or not.

Similarly, an analysis of the relationship between changes in
unionization at the firm level and changes in employment, investment, and output decisions over a twenty-year period found that
unionization reduces employment and sales growth (Bronars and
Deere 1988).

The same authors found that companies facing the threat of unionization protect the wealth of shareholders by issuing instruments
of debt, which effectively reduces the funds available for compensation increases demanded by unions (Bronars and Deere 1991).

How Nonunion Wages Are Determined

To put its compensation philosophy into practice, management
gathers its data primarily targeted on the local labor market; but it
also uses national and other specialized information when relevant.
Comparisons are made with both unionized and unorganized workers. Compensation is structured toward flexibility in work assignment, and therefore it has fewer job classifications and wage grades
than under collective bargaining. In general, as a case study of a
major conglomerate dealing with both unions and unrepresented
employees concluded, important work practices differ significantly
between nonunion and union systems of industrial relations (Verma
1983, p. 170).

The results of the management compensation surveys and proposed changes are then communicated to the employees on company bulletin boards and in meetings. To maintain internal relative wage differentials, periodic job evaluations are also conducted. The following exemplifies how the representative nonunion company presents changes in compensation:

> We are proposing that on [date], all hourly paid employees of the [X] division receive a 3 percent increase in wages while holding the base rate in all hourly occupations at their current levels, with the exception of the Grade [X] level. We also recommend that this increase not be passed on to our customers during this intense period of price concessions and that we attempt to make up the increased costs through productivity gains. In addition to holding the base rate constant, we are proposing that the Grade [X] level be reclassified . . . [because] our spreads have gotten out of proportion and this adjustment will leave us with spreads which are more in line with our . . . counterparts.

The proposed general wage increase was determined on the basis of many factors. The survey covered a local labor market of nine firms, of which four were union, and three that were large firms (including a unit of General Electric). Combined, the other firms employed more than 3,800 employees; the surveying company employed just over 1,100. The surveyed companies had recently increased wages by a weighted average of 3.6 percent, while the three largest had increased wages by 4.76 percent, 4 percent, and 3 percent, respectively. Two smaller companies, both experiencing reduced earnings, gave no general wage increases, although one granted a cost-of-living increase of 1.54 percent. Meanwhile, the Consumer Price Index-W increased over the reference year by 1.2 percent. Throughout the preceding six years within this company, however, total general wage increases had fallen behind the inflation rate. It is also likely that the anticipated gains in productivity would be realized, based on past experience. In terms of recruitment, the proposed increases were expected to retain the company's favorable position in attracting new employees. Its annualized applications for jobs were running at more than three times its workforce and, when coupled with its attrition rate, the company stated that it "can easily and readily recruit any top qualified people for any attrition we experience next year."

The proposal to retain the base rates for classifications of workers (with the one exception) would also make this particular unit of the company comparable with others in the corporation. The unit would still retain its position as a high-wage payer, despite the fact that the freeze of the base rates would make the unit low in the local labor market at entry level positions: ". . . we see no negative impact in supplying highly qualified candidates to fill the needs of the [unit]." Further, the survey went into great detail on the wage rates at all skill levels; the company's rank among others in the area with reference to the hiring rate, unskilled rates, skilled rates, and the rates for the highest paid. The report calculated the weighted average and the variance of wage rates in the local labor market before and after the proposed general wage increase; provided summaries of increases in wage rates in the local labor market; made comparisons between the work unit and other divisions of the company; showed area shift and holiday practices; compared the work unit's labor market with the closest and largest urban labor market; and calculated the estimated financial cost of the proposal. These elaborate procedures and fact-finding indicate that nonunion employers are not one-dimensional pursuers of low wages, who disregard the demand and supply of labor.

Companies using profit sharing detail the method of sharing in the handbook, or a supplemental publication given to all employees. One innovative plan combined profit sharing with features of a pension plan. As long as there are profits, a share determined by the Board of Directors is allocated to the pension plan. The vesting requirement depends on employment with the company or a unit during part of the plan year. Employer contributions are made to an individual account based on the ratio of the employee's eligible compensation to the total eligible compensation of all participants in a plan year. Eligible compensation included all salary, overtime pay, year-end bonuses, and commissions, but excluded severance pay, any special bonuses, and employee contributions to the plan. In addition, the individual participant may contribute a certain percentage of eligible compensation up to a specified maximum. This is maintained in a separate account and is treated as deferred compensation, a 401-K plan. The employee's share can benefit, too, if the profit-sharing trust fund makes profitable investments. Distributions come at retirement or if an employee becomes disabled. The employee's ownership in the fund is also available as a death benefit.

For nonunion companies, quality conditions of employment include a competitive array of other benefit programs. As in their approach to wages, nonunion companies pursue a market approach relying on surveys. Typically, nonunion benefits are generous: "Our benefits program is probably better than most union contracts allow for our area." Although this is a self-serving statement and could not be verified, there is no reason to doubt that benefit programs in the nonunion model are competitive, just as they are in wage compensation.

Recruitment

Human resource management's best technique for attracting quality workers is establishing the company's reputation as a good place to work, whether nonunion or organized. Companies in the nonunion system assert that they try to establish their reputation as good employers as diligently as they strive for a similar reputation for their products. To that end, they interview large numbers of applicants to match applicants to jobs. Nissan reported that it processed 200,000 applications to select just 3,000 workers when it started in Tennessee (Levin 1989).

Typically, new employees are recruited from a number of sources, but companies principally rely on informal ones. Current employees are probably a more important source of recruits among nonunion companies than walk-ins, newspaper advertisements, or employment agencies, private or public. Employment of close relatives of supervisors, managers, or key staff people is discouraged among some companies because of what one employment relations manager termed "inbreeding." Should a family member become a supervisor, the supervisory function is strained. Another drawback is that family disputes may be brought to the workplace.

If the recruitment policy is successful, the employers are the beneficiaries of a labor market que. They are considered preferred employers in the area and attract more applicants than they have vacancies. The advantageous position is accentuated when the area is experiencing high unemployment, such as occurred in the unionized steel industry. In Greenville, Pennsylvania, when jobs and prosperity withered during the 1980s, "a victim of the collapse of steel industry," a nonunion company could report that "we have had the good fortune of having the pick of the crop in this area as other plants are closing or laying off and there are many good people to choose from." This experience was doubtless repeated in Bethlehem, Pennsylvania, when Bethlehem Steel closed its plant there, and is probably occurring as foreign steel imports in the late 1990s further undercut production, especially unionized production, in the United States. On the other hand, where the economy is surging, as in the rebirth of the Philadelphia metropolitan area prior to the 1991 recession and slow recovery, one nonunion company's recruitment became more difficult, but it claimed that its reputation as a good employer enabled it to meet its recruitment targets.

Equal opportunity is standard policy with respect to recruitment, hiring, tenure, training, and promotion among nonunion companies, as under union employers. Adherence to the policy of nondiscrimination is affirmed in applications for employment and in the employees' handbook. Affirmative action programs covering women and minorities are also standard. It is also standard policy to give disabled persons full consideration for any job for which they are qualified, or when hired as trainees. Policy bans harassment of employees and discrimination is a violation of policy and is subject to disciplinary action including discharge.

There are no data to evaluate the nonunion employers' performance on discrimination, but presumably their record matches unionized firms, inasmuch as all are covered by the same federal and state laws. While it is reasonable to believe that the record of the nonunion system is as good as the unionized system's generally, it is certainly better than that of the unionized construction industry, where racial bias has been endemic and historic. It is also axiomatic that discrimination is inconsistent with competitive markets, so inasmuch as nonunion employers function in line with competitive markets, they are financially driven to avoid discrimination, as well as by legal mandates.

In the recruitment process firms evaluate applicants' attitude, stability of employment, prior working relationships with supervisors and co-workers, and overall quality as the criteria in hiring. For an industrial relations system of individual representation, the applicant must come across as one who thinks and speaks for himself. The applicant's propensity for training is also an important factor. If the company is going to invest in the training (the human capital) of its employees, it is motivated to select those in whom the investment will be profitable, for the individual as well as the company. In addition to interviews, the applicant's employment history and personal background are examined. Résumés are required to supplement applications for employment. References are checked and a prehire physical examination is given to candidates for employment. Employment tests are also used as part of the normal hiring procedures. The tests are to reflect job requirements and to match the person to the job. A "good fit" with the company's culture is also a criterion. In seeking the "good fit," nonunion companies stress that the legal requirements of the National Labor Relations Act are strictly observed. Under the act, it is an unfair labor practice for an employer to discourage membership in a labor organization during the course of hiring. In practice, prior membership of an applicant in a union has pluses as well as minuses for the nonunion company, so even if nonunion employers legally attempt to screen out former union members, they may be rejecting good workers. Experience shows that when unionized companies close up because of business failure, many good workers become available, and nonunion companies can benefit from their services.

Applicants are typically interviewed by a member of human resource management staff and the supervisor of the department where a job is available. Although nearly all recruitment goes through the personnel office, there are a few examples in which the recruitment is left to the operating department. The responsibility of human resource management in the new employee's orientation is to cover most of the topics listed in the employees' handbook. Supervisors or department managers deal with job content, customer satisfaction, quality control, and those features of the handbook dealing with miscellaneous personal requirements. Part of the initial interview includes testing to determine skill level. One practice is to avoid hiring at a skill position below that of the applicant's previous experience in order to avoid future discontent. In addition to avoiding employee resentment and frustration, the practice ties into the goal of training new employees in skills specific to the company's needs, and with the expectation that subsequently the employee would be upgraded. After being hired, a common practice is to give new employees a tour of the plant or facility. A typical orientation program for new employees includes:

1. Company history, products and literature.
2. Company labor policy, equal opportunity and affirmative action.
3. Safety, including employee responsibilities.
4. First aid.
5. Explanation of evaluation procedures.
6. Promotion and transfer policy and job opportunity system.
7. Complaint procedures and open door policy.
8. Disciplinary procedures.
9. Explanation of the benefit programs and of procedures for filing claims.
10. Attendance requirements, incentives, pay practices.
11. Sick time, and disability for short- and long-term periods.
12. Holidays including pay practices.
13. Vacations, pay practices, and accumulation and usage.
14. Overtime requirements and pay practice.
15. Company activities.

Periodically, employees are asked to review the orientation procedures and topics covered in order to improve them. Follow-up shows that these reviews have improved both the orientation and hiring procedures. Among representative nonunion firms, new employees are reviewed usually in thirty days, again in six months, and then annually thereafter. After promotion, there is a job review thirty days later.

There are several developments in labor markets that will greatly affect recruitment and strengthen the competitive advantage of the nonunion model. First is the growing part-time labor market. Companies are increasingly hiring part-time and temporary help because of the increased costs of benefit programs and the demand of many in the labor market of the past two decades for part-time work. These employees are advised at the outset that their employment will be limited. This pool of contingent labor is an important part of the profile of the nonunion workforce. Another development in labor markets has been the tightening of the available labor supply in the 1990s. This favors the nonunion more than the organized system of labor relations because of the individual system's greater reliance on part-timers, the physically challenged, retirees, and other potential labor force participants. Another is the growing numbers of former union members, a development of particular interest to the nonunion system of industrial relations. While they widen the potential labor pool, the question is, How will former union members affect labor relations in a nonunion company? Some former union members will surely want to import unionism, but many may be so disillusioned with unions over the loss of their jobs that they may become activists opposing unionization. As already noted, the employment of former union members brings both advantages (in good workers) and disadvantages to the nonunion employer. One of the disadvantages is the union organizing tactic called "salting." Salting is the planting of union sympathizers in the nonunion workforce in hopes of fostering eventual unionization of that workforce.

Training and Promotion

Retention and promotion of employees depend mainly on continuing training because much of human capital is acquired on the job rather than in formal training. Supervisors, together with training staff, are responsible for the development of employees in the individual system of representation. Training for employees is accomplished in several ways and varies between blue-and white-collar workers. For blue-collar workers, training starts with orientation programs and continues with classroom and on-the-job training, apprenticeship training (registered with the state), cross-training among departments, training centers, quality-control instruction, and educational assistance programs. The educational assistance programs offer financial assistance to employees who wish to obtain practical training useful in the current job, in a higher level position, or even to retain the current job. In many instances, the employer reimburses training costs in full.

Some firms whose workforce is predominantly white collar offer in-house training programs resembling college courses not only in content but also in requiring prerequisites. One example offered training for different levels of personnel, and for all employees in personal development and enrichment. Personal development courses include computer programming, computer operation, telemarketing, and management techniques. In personal development, there are courses in achieving one's potential and changing and mastering attitudes toward investment. Some companies encourage and support their white-collar workers to take college or correspondence courses. The company reimburses tuition and fees for courses completed satisfactorily.

The typical policy for promotion provides for an internal job posting and bidding. The factors taken into consideration are ability, competitive experience and seniority, physical fitness, and work records. Competitive seniority is distinguished from a simple longevity of service in that it takes account of merit. All else being equal, seniority will prevail in promotion procedures: "Promotions are based on merit with seniority being given weight in tiebreaker situations." Open positions are posted for a specific number of days; candidates are ranked by seniority, screened for attendance or performance problems, interviewed, and a selection is made based on reasonable qualifications. The treatment of seniority is mixed: at times the qualifications for the new job are virtually equated with seniority: "The person with the most seniority is selected as the best trained, but not always." However, "the significance of seniority is low in considering promotions if the employee has a bad work record," and "employees know that they can be turned down on a promotional sequence if they have an attendance problem," but, "if they improve, they will be considered the next time." In general, there is greater flexibility in administering promotion in the nonunion than in the unionized system of representation.

Employment Security, Turnover, and Transfers

Until the downsizing of the past two decades, the condition that probably attached the worker to the nonunion employer most was probably employment security. Although that attachment was undoubtedly shaken, the image of employment security at nonunion companies remains high in comparison to the staggering losses of employment in the organized sector—steel, autos, clothing, construction, transportation, communication, and mining. If downsizing has affected the attitudes of nonunion workers, white and blue collar, toward the individual system, it has yet to manifest itself in the statistics of unionism and nonunionism. Employment security is prominent in the "pulse taking" of attitude surveys and in employer practices. Low turnover, quits, layoffs, and discharges are the complements to a conscientious recruitment process. Some attribute the low separation rates of nonunion firms to management's fear that it may create a prounion climate if separation rates are high, but this assumes bottomless pockets and an unwillingness to discipline violations. Nonunion companies weathered the steep recession of 1981–1982 when unemployment rates hit levels not seen since the late 1930s, without any upward swing in unionism; in fact nonunionism grew. In contrast, the unionized workforce endured heavy losses during that downturn, losses from which it did not recover during the ensuing recovery, and in the upturn following the 1991 downturn.

A major goal of human resource management under the nonunion system is stabilizing employment in order to retain the company's reputation as a good employer: "Our management firmly believes that the best way to have a stabilized workforce is to restrict the use of layoffs." A company with a nonlayoff policy stated that "in our 50 years of operation, even in less than positive economic conditions, we have maintained full-employment." Nevertheless, low labor turnover in the nonunion sector is not always attainable, especially in a startup or cyclically sensitive industry.

However, quantitative comparisons between comparable unionized and nonunion employers show that employment growth is substantially greater among nonunion companies (Long 1993). Another factor contributing to the stability of employment among nonunion firms is the growing practice of converting hourly paid workers to salaried status. Profit sharing has also become a more common form of compensation among nonunion companies, and this, too, contributes to reduced turnover. One striking example of the relationship of profit sharing, overall compensation, and employment security is the experience of a company which went through bankruptcy and came out of it a reorganized and more competitive company. With better times, it shared profits with employees twice a year and could say that "our employees know what can and can't happen . . . [and] appreciate profit sharing as being a team effort."

Employment security is at the top of the list in collective bargaining relationships as well, but in some it emerged as a belated effort to contain the effects of more competitive product markets. For the UAW, "employment security has emerged as the top collective bargaining priority . . . in the 1980s" (Friedman and Fischer 1988, p. 1). It continues to be a top priority to this time, but two recent developments in the automobile industry will erode the already ebbing ability of the UAW to slow the erosion of jobs in the industry. One is the overcapacity of the industry worldwide, relative to demand. The other is the development of modular construction. Because the industry is a worldwide producer, its productive overcapacity has led to mergers, most notable of Daimler and Chrysler, with more expected to follow soon (Ford and Volvo are a current possibility). Despite denials of intentions of downsizing the workforce, on the grounds that Daimler-Chrysler products are complementary rather than competitive, it is more reasonable to believe economies in employment can be attained at least among white-collar groups.

Modular production is a process that allows the manufacturing of sections of a car to be made outside the main plant for later assembly. It began more than five years ago with a General Motors subsidiary, Delphi Interior and Lighting Systems' "Super Plug" door hardware module. In essence, the Super Plug combines all the disparate car-door components, including wiring, harnesses, door handles, window-guidance channels, stereo speakers, and electric motors into one plastic molding that can be placed inside a door and screwed into place with six fasteners. Clearly, this will reduce the labor requirements and aggravate the already serious loss of membership of the union, once about 1.3 million in numbers, now down to about half that. Modular construction has also led to new suppliers who are nonunion.

Confronted with the mounting pressure of technological change and increased market competition, the UAW retains and seeks to enlarge its "target of a lifetime guaranteed employment" (Friedman and Fischer, 1988 pp. 4, 17–18). The goal would convert labor from a variable to a fixed cost of production, in contrast with nonunion practices, where management still retains its authority to manage the size and deployment of the workforce. Instead of relaxing restrictive work rules, guaranteed lifetime employment under a collective bargaining agreement probably tightens them as unions confront competing job claims from members.

A potential alternative frequently brought forward as a solution to the interests of the two parties in the organized system is cooperation, but it, too, may be insufficient to meet the challenges of an increasingly competitive world market. Thus, following is an assessment of the UAW's defeat at Nissan: "While American auto makers and the union have been moving toward more cooperation in a new economic climate, the vote at Nissan indicates they will have to come up with more innovative ways to meet the more competitive challenge of foreign companies who have shown they can beat [organized] American manufacturers at their own game, with American workers" (Levin 1989). The writer who penned that assessment neglected to identify a determined group, a minority within the UAW, the New Directions group, which bitterly opposes any cooperative arrangements with management as a "sell-out" of the members. Actually, the position of the leadership of the UAW is not much different from that of the dissidents. It favors union-management cooperation, but declared that while its goal, "the protection of the members' welfare," was the union's problem, the "profitability of the company is the company's problem" (Levin 1989). As we head toward the new century, who is to say that the ideas of the New Directions group will be forgotten? In fact, the once affiliated Canadians branch of the UAW prides itself on practices that embody the ideology of the New Directions group in the United States.

Policies on layoffs and recall in the individual system are similar to those under collective bargaining. When layoffs in nonunion establishments occur, seniority applies both in separations and in recall. Recall is in reverse order of a layoff. One company's policy on layoffs states: "We go as near as possible to provide absolute job protection against business cycles, competition, and changes in the customers' taste . . . we are reluctant to lay off." Another has a rule that after ten years of employment the signature of the president is required to lay off an employee. The rule is unwritten, but it is common knowledge among employees. Another company reported that although it has no written policy on employment security, "our employees know we won't lay off except for the survival of the company. We haven't laid off in the past fifteen years. That's a good record for the steel industry." During layoffs, companies have extended insurance (including health) programs to cover their former employees during part of any long-term unemployment. Severance compensation is paid if the layoff is permanent.

Companies believe their communication systems and their flexibility in work assignment keeps turnover low. Because of their commitment to avoid layoffs, nonunion companies believe that their "employees [have] a greater commitment and dedication to the company and a heightened realization of job security." A company in metals manufacturing reported that, despite its cyclical sensitivity, it had not used its layoff procedures for many years. Given the labor market conditions since, it is likely that the policy remains intact. In the past, when that company did experience cutbacks in production, the affected employees were reassigned to other, nonproduction jobs within the company. Another company that normally experiences cyclical fluctuations in sales and shipments has smoothed its layoff problems by similar procedures in assigning employees to other departments within the plant. Another example in paper manufacturing reported that "employment security has always been a major concern for us. We practice a no-layoff attitude . . . and this has encouraged our people to accept a wide variety of assignments outside of their normal work skill and has created a very flexible and broadly trained employee base." These practices are not unique to the nonunion system but are much easier to implement than in the organized sector. In organized companies, the employer may have to negotiate with a union other than the representative of its employees about doing maintenance work when production is cut back for business reasons. At the Big Three auto makers, job classifications prevent assembly workers from doing more complicated work, such as maintaining machines, or less skilled work, such as cleaning floors around their work areas (Levin 1989).

In industries that experience large seasonal expansions, such as retailing, temporary employees supplement the extension of working time of part-timers to fill staffing requirements. This avoids layoffs of regular employees in less busy seasons. In addition, both productivity gains and avoiding layoff are enhanced by management's ability to modify work schedules and to assign work, measures that help sustain employment security. Human resource management contrasts the flexibility in work assignment among nonunion companies with the more rigid unionized system which limits work assignment or even requires that work be given to outside unionized workers with the recognized jurisdictional claim. On work assignment, the Nissan workers said, "we're pretty free to do our jobs the way we want to and to make suggestions" (Levin 1989). Workers learn to perform different tasks and use a more flexible seniority system to allocate work. These practices dovetail smoothly with structures of employee participation (Chapter 7). In contrast, rotation is often problematic in the organized system because of job classifications spelled out in collective bargaining agreements.

Flexibility in work assignments in the nonunion system not only preserves jobs but enhances productivity. One company cited an example of flexibility and productivity as follows: "A specific instance in our company is where we have large earth hauling trucks that will require 15–20 minutes to load. A driver will park the truck at the quarry face, then jump into another truck and drive it to the crusher while the first truck is unloaded. This would be unheard of in a unionized shop." Another example of management flexibility in changing work schedules that increased productivity while minimizing turnover is the following:

> [Several] years ago, work schedules were revised resulting in annual savings of 116,000 work hours, improved customer service and reduced training costs. Although this major shift in schedules affected about 1,350 people, at the end of six months there were [only] five who chose not to accept the change and decided to leave the company—four of the five did this by taking early retirement.

The success of the change was attributed to communicating the details to the employees through supervisors and higher management well in advance of the change. The financial necessities for the change were explained, and every employee affected was interviewed in order to deal with their concerns.

Temporary transfer policies are designed to maintain efficiency and production, but may also be motivated for reasons of training, avoiding personality conflicts, and health and other personal situations. During the transfer, the employee is paid at the old rate for the new job, more if it is a higher paying job, and after a period (thirty days, for example), at a lower rate for a less skilled position. Technological displacements are handled as far as possible through normal attrition. Overtime is relied upon before new employees are hired. For those who are laid off, there is a practice to reinstate the employee, if rehired within six months of layoff, with the original hire date determining the person's eligibility for all benefits, except accrual of paid time-off for the period of the layoff. Prior to the federal legislation on closures, the typical policies provided severance pay and the opportunity to relocate to other facilities.

Safety

The Occupational Safety and Health Act (OSHA) requires employers to provide a safe and healthy work environment. Nonunion employers are no less committed to safety than their unionized counterparts, although there have been conspicuous exceptions.

As any responsible management will do, the nonunion management investigates every accident or incident involving safety and acts promptly. When hired, employees are given literature on safety and health. The importance of safety in the nonunion model was highlighted in the representation election at Nissan in July 1989. The only major antiemployer issue that the UAW could identify were inadequate safety measures in the plant. The employees themselves resolved the problem, depriving the UAW of its principal issue. The problem arose from a method of shooting screws into the cars' steering column while employees were seated on the floor, causing carpal tunnel syndrome. A committee of employees, in collaboration with an outside consultant, found a special drill that was capable of preventing the disorder. The new drill cost $1,400, replacing an older drill worth $400. And, as already noted, the union lost the election, despite its challenge of the company's safety record.

Among nonunion companies, safety and health programs are frequently administered by joint committees of employees and managerial personnel, either the supervisor or personnel manager. Employee membership on the committees rotates so as eventually to include the entire work force. Safety committees are usually established under the employees' handbook. They are expected to contribute ideas to improve safety, to provide safety education, to detect unsafe conditions and hazards, and to recommend corrective measures. If special protective clothing or appliances are required, companies either assist or cover all costs. Employees are required to observe safety rules and to report any injury or unsafe condition to the supervisor. Violation of safety rules can result in disciplinary action, including discharge.

Drug and alcohol abuse are issues common to the workplace under both systems of representation. In the nonunion system, management and supervisors are trained to recognize the symptoms of drug and alcohol abuse and handle potential resistance and aggression. The same is true of organized companies. Employees receive an explanation of the company's policies and its programs of rehabilitation. The training on substance abuse comes from both in-house and outside experts. Another important feature of employee relations in some nonunion systems is an employee assistance program for those having psychological problems. An employee and family members having personal problems can receive professional assistance at no charge. Costs outside the program are usually offset, in part, by the benefit program. Retired workers are also often covered. In general, the conditions of employment in the nonunion system, except for compensation, parallel those in the organized system. The convergence can be attributed to rational behavior, to markets, and to government policies and legislation.

——— Seven ———

Is There a Third Way?

The Nonunion Employee Representation Model

The thesis of this book is that there are only two alternatives to employee-employer relations in the United States: the individual system and the organized system. However, a group of academic specialists has recently argued that another model, which they call Nonunion Employee Representation, or NER (Kaufman and Taras 1999), is an alternative to the organized system and, although they did not note it, presumably to individual representation as well. Is their concept a third alternative in employee-employer relations? In brief, I reject the hypothesis.

Although I have used the term nonunion system of representation from time to time in this book, I used it as a synonym for the model of the individual system of employee representation. In its various versions, NER, as presented by its authors, is a *collective form of representation*, a form of "shadow unionism." All versions of NER engage to some extent in collective representation; and some engage in negotiation over the terms and conditions of employment. The authors of NER define Nonunion Employee Representation as

> routinized forums in which nonunion employees meet with management to discuss issues pertaining to the terms and conditions of employment, at either the plant or enterprise level. (Taras and Copping 1998)

Inasmuch as all these "routinized forums" are established by employers, they are illegal in the United States. Under some jurisdictions in Canada, however, NER is legal. Hence, the definition applies to Canada, not to the United States. Under the National Labor Relations Act, any labor organization established by the employer is illegal when it deals with the terms and conditions of employment. Under the National Labor Relations Act, when a group of employees meet with management to discuss terms and conditions of employment in fulfillment of their right to self-organization and bargaining, the group is not an NER but a local independent or a local union affiliated with a standard national or international union. When groups of unrepresented employees go to an employer with grievances, however, such as Harris and Associates reported (1984) and as I report in this study, the employees are acting as a spontaneous and temporary group, not a permanent or routinized forum organization such as conceived by NER.

Historically, the groups closest to NER were the employee representation plans of the pre–New Deal years (Chapter 3). These organizations were dismantled—disestablished—by the National Labor Relations Board as illegal institutions violating the rights of workers to self-organization for purposes of collective bargaining and other concerted activities. Disestablishment was and remains the National Labor Relations Board's (NLRB) remedy for eliminating organizations that it decides are employer dominated. By disestablishment, the board sought to restore the status ante quo, that is, the labor relationship that existed prior to the employer's commission of the unfair labor practice. Punishment by fine or imprisonment has never been a remedy for unfair labor practices committed either by employers or unions under the act. Once disestablished, the tainted organization could never appear on the ballot of an NLRB representation election. It could continue only in some social capacity, such as a sports team.

Currently, the closest approximations to NER in the United States are employee participation plans. These plans are established by employers, but what they do and how they do it distinguish them from NER. To begin with, even their names highlight the differences. Employee participation means that employees participate in the production process; they do not represent workers, and that is the vital distinction. The raison d'être for employee participation is to increase the productivity, the quality of output, and the competitiveness of the firm; it excludes representation for purposes of bargaining or any other collective purpose. Economic analysis sets these plans apart: employee participation deals with the production function, that is, how to produce. NERs, while sharing the goal of enhancing efficiency, go beyond the production function and participate in the *governance* of the workplace, just like unions, or as the historical employee representation plans in the pre–New Deal era. NER, as its proponents state, deals with the "traditional bread and butter concerns of employees, such as wages, benefits, hours and job security" (Kaufman and Taras 1999, p. 11). Although a disclaimer is added, stating that these subjects are less frequently handled by nonunion representational groups, their activities transform them into "shadow unions," which is not lawful in this country. Those NERs that do not deal with the terms and conditions of employment but engage in "collective representation," enabling "employees . . . the ability and venue to make their collective needs known to management" (Kaufman and Taras 1999, p. 8), also do not escape the ban of the law, since making "collective needs known to management" is collective representation. In my view, any form of NER would have to transform itself into a union, whether a local independent or a local affiliated with a national or international union. In fact, that is what occurred in thousands of instances, especially in the early days of the New Deal. Numerous employee representation plans established by employers that fell short of the NLRB's finding of domination (i.e., found to be illegally assisted but not dominated by employers and could therefore survive once purged of illegal employer assistance) were transformed into unions, affiliated or independent.

Canadian labor law (federal and provincial) is modeled on the National Labor Relations Act but is much more supportive of unions. Oddly, it did not adopt the ban on employer-dominated labor organizations prevailing in the United States. This surprising development can be attributed to several factors, but the most important is probably the influence of Canadian Prime Minister William McKenzie King. He was prime minister of Canada at the time (1944) when the federal government promulgated Privy Council Order

1003, which established Canada's labor policies for both federal and provincial governments during World War II. The order was modeled on the American experience except for the ban on employer-controlled labor organizations. The reason for its exclusion was King's belief that they contributed to industrial peace, based on his earlier experience in labor relations in the United States and Canada as a consultant to John D. Rockefeller. After the war, the provincial governments adopted their own labor laws, and some, at least, continued to exclude the prohibition of employer-controlled labor organizations as an unfair labor practice. Because of that quirk of history, employer-sponsored organizations survived in some Canadian jurisdictions, which led to the concept of Nonunion Employee Representation (Taras 1997) as a legal institution in Canada.

Is There a Representation Gap?

Another perspective on the possibility of a "third way" in workers' representation emerges from the question, What do workers want? In response to their own question, presented at the fiftieth annual labor conference in 1998, sponsored by New York University, Richard Freeman and Joel Rogers contended that workers want voice, representation, and power in the American workplace, currently absent because there is a representational gap in the private labor market. According to them, workers in the private economy want organized representation, whether by union, works' councils (referred to as joint committees), or an undefined and therefore vague form of independent organization to fill the representation gap in the American workplace (Freeman and Rogers 1997, pp. 10, 24). Individual representation was not one of the alternatives in their survey. Almost unspoken, their preference is for unions, but faced by what I call a future in the "twilight zone" (Chapter 8), Freeman and Rogers are prepared to accept works' councils as a preliminary step to eventual reunionization.

To establish the existence of the representational gap, the coauthors asked, first, "Do employees want greater participation and representation [in decision making] at their workplace than is currently provided?" Their finding was yes, they do, and that it was by a "vast majority." Not to put too fine a point on it, wouldn't it have been not only logical but more intellectually defensible to express what the authors meant by "influence," and what employees thought "influence" meant in the workplace? It also would have been preferable if the employees were asked whether they wished to participate at all in decision making, desired no change, or wished to participate less in workplace governance. Although these things were not asked directly, in fact, Freeman and Rogers did find, despite the question as framed, that more than one-third would keep their role in the workplace unchanged, 1 percent wanted less participation. As they reported them, the findings are confusing, even contradictory.

Thus, the attitude of the two-thirds desiring more influence is inconsistent with another and associated finding, that up to 81 percent of those surveyed were satisfied (very satisfied and satisfied) with their general role in the governance of the workplace. When the survey identified specific subjects on which employees might wish to exercise more influence, those reporting satisfaction changed little, ranging now from 67 to 81 percent. As to how much influence was desired in those specific areas of decision making, the reader is asked to accept such characterizations as "having a lot of influence" and "a lot of direct involvement."

As their second question Freeman and Rogers wanted to know how nonunion, nonmanagerial employees felt about employee involvement programs as structures to improve productivity or quality of output. A total of 86 percent of the respondents found them effective (very effective and somewhat effective). In assessing the responses on effectiveness, however, the authors wrote that "only" 31 percent rated them highly and "only" 55 percent viewed them as somewhat effective, but forgot their adverbial qualification when describing the 11 percent of employees who found the employee participation programs "ineffective." (Freeman and Rogers 1997, p. 6). Similarly, on employees' voice, the authors wrote that "only" 28 percent regarded their company's voice system as very effective, and 49 percent judged it somewhat or not too effective; but again, there was no qualification on the 21 percent who judged their employer's voice system as "not effective at all." (There is apparently a typographical error in the authors' report at this point; after noting that 28 percent of employees rated their system of voice very effective, the next phrase reports a 70 percent rate as somewhat effective, followed by, in parenthesis, "49 percent," and then, the phrase "or not too effective at all (21) percent." I believe the authors intended to report percentages of 20, 49, and 21, respectively.) Further on employee voice, Freeman and Rogers reported that 74 percent of employees rated their employers' "open door, town meeting, and the like," as effective (very and somewhat effective); 19 percent classified them as not effective; and 7 percent did not respond. In other words, even though employees see value in employee participation programs and employers' policies on employee voice, they had considerable participation in the workplace. According to Freeman and Rogers, they want more power in decision making (p. 16).

For the sake of argument, let us assume that the authors are correct in their finding that a "vast majority" of workers demand more power in decision making in the workplace than they now have. Two questions follow: How many does a "vast majority" of employees translate into numerically? And, whatever the number, does it matter in the real labor market? For answers, we must turn first to an earlier report (1993) by the same authors on nonunion employee representation, and to the fact-finding report of the Dunlop Commission of May 1994, of which Freeman was a member.

In their earlier report, Freeman and Rogers (1993) claimed that the representational gap could number 80 million wage and salaried workers. At that time, this would constitute nearly the entire private-sector employment that was nonunion. On the other hand, the fact-finding Dunlop Commission estimated that 40 million private nonunion and more than 9 million union workers wanted to participate in decision making at their workplace (U.S. Department of Labor and U.S. Department of Commerce 1994a, p. 52). The Commission reiterated, now in relative rather than absolute figures, the representational gap as "63 percent of employees say they want more influence, compared to 35 percent who are content with things as they are" (U.S. Department of Labor and U.S. Department of Commerce 1994b, p. 64).

Based on these and other findings, a majority of the Commission recommended legalization of employee participation programs that deal with productivity, not representation (see below), in exchange for legislation that would also redefine supervisors as employees within the meaning of the law, giving them the right to join unions. The Commission also recommended vigorous enforcement of the law against employer-dominated unions. Both were appended to the majority recommendation to legalizing employee participation as a way of softening the opposition of the unions and their representative on the Commission. The recommendation to change the status of supervisors was a major effort to accommodate the unions because supervisors are regarded (and rightly so) as major obstacles to organizing production workers (Chapter 5). Management opposed this move vigorously because of its experience with unions of supervisors during and shortly after World War II. Their opposition led to the amendment in the Taft-Hartley Act that defined the supervisory occupation in language that exempted them from coverage under the act. Shortly thereafter, unions of supervisors disappeared. Under current law, supervisors could still unionize, but employers could discharge them without violating the act because they are not employees within the meaning of the act and therefore are not protected if they choose to unionize.

Majority support for employee participation programs also may have also included some members who believed that structures of employee participation could be a step toward unionism. That theory held that nonunion workers would become acclimated to a collective form of communication with employers, and this would eventually lead to a formal membership organization (a union). That assumption echoes a recommendation to the AFL-CIO by some academics (some of whom were also members of the Commission) that it set up "associations" of nonunion workers who would be eligible for the Federation's benefits program, a credit card, and access to counselors on legal and financial matters, in the expectation that their participation would lead these nonunion workers to join a union. The program failed, and union membership and density continued to fall. Likewise, I do not expect employee participation programs to become halfway houses to unions. Evidently the Commission's union member, Douglas A. Fraser, a former president of the United Auto Workers (UAW), did not see it that way either and dissented from the majority. His dissent is as interesting as it is important because it was a reiteration of the historic gulf that has often separated outside advisers from union practitioners. To unionists, employee participation programs, like the employee representation plans and company unions of the past, are obstacles to unionization.

The reason workers' demand for representation goes unfilled, according to Freeman and Rogers, is employer opposition (Freeman and Rogers 1997, pp. 17, 18, 19). This has been their explanation, and that of many others, over the past two decades. Paul Weiler, however, one of the originators of the claim that employers' opposition was responsible for the representation gap, finally averred that "most employers still do fight within the legal rules of the contest" and that "our national labor law still states that employees can have union representation and collective bargaining if they want it . . . but they must *really* want the benefits of that institution" (Weiler 1988; emphasis in the original).

Over time, however, the academics who identified the representation gap changed the identity of the institution that was to fill the gap. Until the 1990s, the gap was to be filled by a revival of union representation. Early in the 1990s, Weiler and others began to advocate mandatory works' councils, instead of unions, to fill the gap. Freeman and Rogers followed that lead, as they and others had followed Weiler's original identification of unions as the proper institution to fill the representational void. The probability of Congress's adopting mandatory works' councils in the United States is nil.

Does the claimed desire of nonunion employees for more "influence" have any significance in the labor market? In short, no. Economists have long distinguished between "demand" (desire) and "effective demand (desire made effective by payment)." Demand embodies a wish, while effective demand expresses the consumer's actual willingness to purchase a product or service at various prices. In this case, are nonunion workers ready to pay the costs; are they prepared to vote for organizing unions? The difference between the two concepts of demand is the difference between an ephemeral wish and a readiness to act. In a different way,

Freeman and Rogers acknowledged this reality themselves in a previous article on nonunion representation, by comparing it to what they called the "[Ross] Perot Poll Phenomenon," which they explained meant "people saying something sounds good without knowing its content" (Freeman and Rogers 1993, pp. 28–29). Their own distinction shakes the foundation of their claim that "a vast majority" want more influence in the workplace. It also shakes their claim for the existence of a representation gap.

Assuming, again, that the Freeman-Rogers's finding of a representation gap is accurate, how is it to be closed? In their previous article (but absent in the more recent report), they wrote that "democratic principles argue for [the] establishment" of some form of employee representation (Freeman and Rogers 1993, p.65). Before reiterating their answer to the gap in representation, the validity of their supposition that "democratic principles argue for some form of representation" must be challenged. They have only their own survey, and this "evidence" is contradicted by the results of NLRB elections, which measure what I have called effective demand (Chapter 8).

For them, the gap-filler doubtless means works' councils, echoing Weiler's call for them. And although they did not identify who would establish these structures of representation, only Congress and the president are capable of creating them, and the Supreme Court of validating them. Meantime, what of the benefits to costs ratio of works' councils? According to Freeman and Rogers, the benefits of the works' councils outweigh their costs, as the experience of Western European countries and Japan show (Freeman and Rogers 1993, pp.14, 66). However, that conclusion is not universally accepted as fact. For example, they ignored the high German unemployment rate, which must be linked, in part, to the cost of works' councils.

Another way to analyze the representation gap is the difference between the percentage of nonunion workers who say they would vote for union representation and the percentage of private-sector workers who actually are in unions, a procedure that supporters of unions have from time to time invoked. Even though a minority of all workers wanted union representation as reported by surveys

(Chapters 1 and 4), approximately one-third to 40 percent do want unions. This number greatly exceeds actual levels of density in the private sector, now just about 9 percent, and is seen as a huge untapped reservoir of union members. Currently that could translate into three to more than a fourfold increase in market share and a huge gain in membership, as much as 27 million new union members. But are these figures realistic? Union organizers confront a different (real) world from that suggested by these academic speculations. While NLRB representation elections require only a 30 percent showing of interest by workers to initiate the election procedure, union organizers rarely if ever petition for one with such a small showing. Thus, to treat the gap between potential and actual membership as a real measure of the representation gap is more than optimistic.

There is another and paradoxical perspective of the representation gap, this one from the viewpoint of nonunion employers. Why is employer opposition to unionization so ineffective in NLRB elections compared to survey findings? Over the last quarter century, unions have scored an average win rate of about 50 percent in organizing elections, compared to survey results that show results favoring individual representation ranging above 60 percent? Could employer tactics to avoid unions be less effective than they and the public believe? The discrepancy lies in the unions' selection of elections they are most likely to win, which indicates that petitions for a representation election must be based on more than the minimum legal requirement of 30 percent of the potential voters in the proposed bargaining unit. Because unions will customarily only seek an election when they have more than one-half of the prospective worker-voters who have signed cards, their loss rate is lower than the surveys would forecast.

Based on votes for no union (individual representation), throughout more than the past quarter century (1970–1997), nonunion workers voted for no union at rates below the Harris/Michigan/Freeman and Rogers numbers, and just under the Lipset/Meltz survey figure of 60 percent. The average percentage of votes in previously unorganized units for no union (individual representation) over the past quarter century was more than 50 percent (Chapter 7). Instead of a gap in organized representation, could the argument be reversed. Could there be a gap between nonunion workers' demand for individual representation in actual elections and the potential indicated by the various surveys?

Employee Participation Plans

Employee participation plans or programs, a recent development in labor relations, do not fill the alleged representation gap, nor are they an alternative to unions or the individual system. They are also not an Nonunion Employee Represesntation (NER) in the United States, as advocates of NER apparently contend (Estreicher 1998). They consist of several types or forms: Some deal directly with the production function, for example, quality circles, team-based work structures, and joint task forces on production issues which are empowered to make decisions affecting how the work would be done. Some affect production indirectly through committees concerned with safety and health in the workplace (which also are recognized for their intrinsic human values). Other structures of employee participation focus on human capital investment, which includes joint labor-management training programs and information-sharing forums. In sum, employee participation deals primarily with technological issues, issues focusing on better ways of producing goods or furnishing services, not on the governance of the workplace. These are the quintessential features of employee participation structures.

Employee participation programs were characterized recently in these terms:

> Neither employers nor employees typically regard employee participation arrangements as being the functional equivalent of a union, but one which is set up and paid for by the employer . . . [arising] out of management enlightened self interest . . . in promoting organizational and financial health. (Leibowitz 1997, p. 2)

Increased competition in marketplaces worldwide, "the birth and burgeoning of microelectronic technology, and the incredibly short product life cycles" spurred organizational changes in the work place to improve productivity and one of these was the establishment of employee participation programs (Leibowitz 1997, p. 1).

Michael H. LeRoy's surveys of employee involvement found that most in his sample had formally stated goals, that most addressed efficiency, and that these fell within legally permissible employer-employee activity. He found that these plans could and did recommend or implement action plans on a wide array of tasks and responsibilities for the purposes of improving the quantity and quality of output. Among these actions were upgrading the skills of employees, improving the production function (the technology of how to produce), creating a uniform and consistent production process, reducing the time needed to develop new products and add them to the firm's product line in a way to gain customer satisfaction, and improving the mesh between the assembly and testing of products. Employee participation groups also could recommend policy changes to human resource management. They contribute to how to market the company's products and develop methods that would learn what consumers thought of the product or service. Their interest in the customer reflects the basic principal of derived demand in economics: employment is derived from consumers' demand for the company's products, as a chain of reasoning employers in the nonunion labor market regularly emphasizes. The results of these activities were found overwhelmingly to have improved productivity, the primary goal of programs of employee participation. This finding was also consistent with the National Labor Relations Board's decisions in the *Electromation* and *Dupont* cases, even though the board declared them illegal labor organizations in these cases (LeRoy 1997, pp. 17–27). LeRoy also found that most of his sample interacted with other work teams and, in a few cases, with customers.

Employee participation programs fit well with and could greatly strengthen the individual system of representation. They expand the range of individual actions contributing to the output of the firm. Although geared to the production and not the representation function, these programs are now under a legal cloud. At this time, employee participation plans are in a legal no-man's land. Several plans have been declared in violation of the National Labor Relations Act as employer-dominated labor organizations and have been disestablished (Electromation 1992, 1993; Dupont 1993), but many continue to function. Which are legal and which are not depends on the facts of the case and the board's doctrines at the time. One factor involved in finding them illegal was that some programs included managerial or supervisory staff. In some cases, the members from management were volunteers; in others, there was no management presence; while in one location, employees selected the management member of the work team.

Many continue to function as employers seek the right side of the fine line separating legal from illegal employee participation programs. Either way, in the United States employee participation cannot be equated with NER. If the board was correct in its disestablishment of several plans because they actually dealt with "traditional bread and butter concerns of employees, such as wages benefits, hours and job security," as NERs are said to do (Kaufman and Taras 1999, p. 11), then they cannot be a form of NER. Those that continue to function legally must necessarily fail to meet the definition and practice of an NER.

Congress has attempted to clarify the legal ambiguities on employee participation, but presidential vetoes, actual and threatened, have stymied the proposed reform legislation, known as the Teamwork for Employees and Managers (TEAM) Act. President Clinton has opposed the enactment of the reforms at the behest of organized labor, which regards employee participation plans as obstacles to organizing. The proposed TEAM act would legalize any organization of employees and participating management that addresses matters of quality, productivity efficiency, safety and health, but that denies the organization the right to become the employees' exclusive bargaining representative and to negotiate the terms and conditions of employment. If it becomes law eventually, not only would employee participation plans be legitimized, but some forms of NER could qualify as well.

The proposed TEAM act, as viewed by employers, recognizes the dramatic difference between the American economy of the pre–World War II days and the past several decades. The National Labor Relations Act was adopted in the preinformation age and when the attitudes of both employers and workers, and the nature of work and technology, were substantially different from today. Labor laws were written for a different work environment and therefore lag the changes that have altered how work is now done. The workforce and workplace of today need the flexibility that provides individualized solutions to such issues as scheduling and the pace of work, as well as technical talent different from the 1930s, the era of the company-dominated labor organization. During the earlier period, the economy was largely a closed one, especially after the enactment of the Smoot-Hawley tariff act in 1930. Now, the American economy is the major player in world trade, commerce, and finance; it is an open economy. The policies of the NLRB dealt with a different workforce (mostly blue collar) and different labor organizations (the company-dominated union), so today these policies lag market developments, technological change, and labor relations realities of the late twentieth century. American workers and employers require labor relations practices and structures that are compatible with the New Age of Adam Smith, not those born in the age of mercantilist controls and regulations. In the end, many disputes over employee participation pit legalistic against efficiency concepts, the past against the future.

Employee participation plans would also add to the communications system in the individual system of representation (Chapter 5) and contribute to its durability. LeRoy's study concluded that most plans of employee participation, in carrying out their primary tasks of enhancing productivity, also improve employee-employer communications. The various forums of employee participation supply information about the performance, strategy, and mission of the company, knowledge that would enable employees to understand and contribute to the competitive performance of the company. Employee participation plans would strengthen the individual system because they emphasize the contribution of individual workers to production and communication. Necessarily, this also heightens the value of each individual to the competitive success of the company, as well as to individual representation.

Employee participation plans are also empirically applying a basic theory of labor economics, the theory of marginal productivity. This theory is built upon the contribution of individual workers to output. Empirically, this is recognized in the distribution of compensation through gain and profit sharing, bonuses that supplement the traditional hourly rate, thereby distinguishing between qualitative differences in the workforce. A study of Canadian small businesses reported conclusions on managements' motives that would apply below the border as well:

> Profit sharing was seen [by CEOs] as either a way to increase company performance, through "improving employee motivation," "promoting teamwork," and "helping employees understand the business," or a way to provide better rewards to employees, thus increasing their loyalty and commitment to the firm ("reward loyal employees," "improve compensation package," "retain employees," "build employee commitment"). (Long 1997, p. 727)

Long also reported that the CEOs in his sample did not "appear to see profit sharing as a weapon for weakening or avoiding the union." (Long 1997 p. 727). On the other hand, profit sharing has not only become more widespread in nonunion companies but reinforces the basic concept and practice of the individual system of representation.

Employee participation plans alter the structure of the workplace from the traditional vertical or hierarchical (top-down) to a horizontal or "flat" structure. The "flat" structure not only offers a new and more efficient arrangement to improve the competitive position of the business; by accentuating the contribution of individual workers, it can also alter the traditional relationship between employers and employees, from a hierarchical to the horizontal relationship. So, in promoting the efficiency of the production function, employee participation also reinforces individualism in the representation function.

The current extent of employee participation programs is unknown. They were probably introduced into the nonunion sector during the 1970s (McMahan and Lawler 1994, p. 3). The organized sector's experience with labor-management cooperation preceded employee participation, if experience under employee representation plans in the pre–New Deal era is excluded. Under the impact of competition, the New Age of Adam Smith, both participation programs and unionized labor-management cooperation became increasingly widespread. By the early 1990s, there were more than 30,000 programs of employee participation involving more than 80 percent of Fortune 1,000 companies (Potter 1991, p. 1). Seven years later, the same figure, 30,000, was reported in another study, suggesting that no new survey had been done (LeRoy 1997, p. 32).

An AFL-CIO report on the new American workplace downplays the prevalence of employee participation plans, however, citing the finding of the 1990 Brock-Marshall Commission on the Skills of the American Workforce that fewer than 5 percent of all employers had established "a high performance" work organization. Another estimate from the Work in America Institute put the number even lower. The AFL-CIO also cited the institute as stating that these organizations were concentrated in Fortune 1,000 companies (AFL-CI0 1994, p. 13).

The Commission on the Future of Worker-Management Relations, appointed by the Clinton administration in the spring of 1993, reported that employee participation (which it identified with the non-union sector), and labor-management cooperation (its term for the union sector) had both increased in number and together accounted for from one-fifth to one-third of the workforce. No breakdown between the two sectors was reported (U.S. Department of Labor and U.S. Department of Commerce 1994, p. 45). In its final report, a majority of the commission endorsed employee participation:

> Where employee participation is sustained over time and integrated with other organization policies and practices, the evidence suggests it generally improves economic performance. If more widely diffused and sustained over time, employee participation and labor management cooperation may contribute to the nation's competitiveness and standard of living. (U.S. Department of Labor and U.S. Department of Commerce 1994, p. 56)

Its support was tepid, however. By the time of the commission's statement, the NLRB's ban on a few employee participation plans had been made and was upheld by the courts (1993), so when the commission addressed the question of a legal remedy to rescue what it acknowledged was beneficial to workers' living standards and to the economy, it did not advocate the legal steps that would be required. Instead, it asked:

> With respect to future legal policy, the major question is whether, and if so, how, the National Labor Relations Act should be revised or interpreted to permit nonunion firms to develop one or more of the array of employee participation plans that have been challenged under Section 8(a)(2) of the Act? (U.S. Department of Labor and U.S. Department of Commerce 1994, pp. 56–57).

Meantime, the NLRB's decisions outlawing structures of employee participation in several cases, probably slowed their formation. Nevertheless, many employers continue to introduce them in the expectation that they meet the criteria that would enable them to pass legal muster (LeRoy 1997). Consequently, according to the AFL-CIO's report on the New American workplace, "the overwhelming majority of workplaces are still operated along traditional lines and likely will continue that way for a very long time"(AFL-CIO 1994, p. 13). Since that does appear to be the case, employee communication under the individual system will continue to go primarily through the traditional routes and continue mainly to address questions arising out of the governance of the workplace, the terms and conditions of employment.

How Employee Participation Could Enhance the Individual System of Representation

Assuming that employee participation will not receive legal sanction, is it essential to the individual system of labor relations? In a word, no. With or without structures of employee participation, the individual system's fewer work rules (lower unit costs of production) will continue to give it a competitive advantage over the organized system. However, the individual system increases its competitive advantage over the organized system with employee participation programs, and that is one of the reasons unions oppose them.

Because some contemporary programs of employee involvement have been declared illegal, it may be thought that they are essentially the same as pre–New Deal structures of employee representation. While they share the attribute of being the result of employers' actions, they nevertheless differ significantly in their functions. Employee representation plans had a long history, dating back to the nineteenth century and from World War I labor policies of the (first) War Labor Board. After a brief postwar decline, they received another boost when employers introduced them in the 1920s as alternatives to unionism. Later still, many were converted by their employers into formal membership organizations, company unions, in response to Sections 7(a) and (b) of the National Industrial Recovery Act of 1933. Most were wiped out by the NLRB as employer violations of the Wagner Act of 1935. While the employee representation plans and the company union were designed to represent employees in a manner and on subjects prescribed by employers, the contemporary legal plans of employee participation avoid activities involving representation dealing with the terms and conditions of employment.

Instead of representational functions, research studies have reported that employee participation plans are "related to a philosophical makeover aimed at instilling high performance work practices" (LeRoy 1997, p. 6). LeRoy cited reports of the Department of Labor that found "many positive outcomes associated with participatory management programs" (LeRoy 1997, p. 8). As a result, employee turnover has been reduced, and profitability, unit productivity, and product quality have improved (LeRoy 1987, p. 6); thereby, the plans have enhanced customer satisfaction with the product or service. The contributions to more and better production and the "flat" organizational structure that is part of employee participation programs have been criticized because of changes in plans and the turnover of employees involved in the plans. Apparently, the turnover referred to is about the impermanence of the structures. Actually, their temporary nature argues against considerations of illegality. Very likely, the turnover is the result of new products and methods of production (the purpose of establishing participatory programs in the first instance) and not of inherent instability in the plans themselves. Instead, the turnover should be regarded as reasonable because, as Leibowitz (1997) wrote, of the incredibly short product life cycles. The turnover reflects changing technological and market conditions, a key to remaining competitive. It also offers more workers the opportunity to gain experience with newer methods of production, a boon to the individual system of representation. Perhaps the criticism reveals a reverence for the security of work rules over experimentation and efficiency inherent in employee participation programs.

Employee Participation and the Organized System

Organized labor is opposed to programs of employee participation and has denied their effectiveness:

> To a greater or lesser extent, such programs may generate more individual worker participation than exists in traditional work organizations. But these "feel-good" programs and these "involvement" or "empowerment" programs which emanate from management and which stop at the task level cannot, by definition, provide workers with any real power over their working lives. Rather, these systems subordinate workers to management in essentially the time-tested ways that have proved wanting. At bottom, then, these programs are a mirage: they offer the appearance, but not the substance, of genuine worker involvement. (AFL-CIO 1994, p. 10)

The AFL-CIO's model of employee participation would consist of five elements, and these match its model of labor-management cooperation in the organized sector:

1. A "fundamental redistribution of decision-making authority from management to teams of workers."

2. Redesigning jobs "to include a greater variety of skills and tasks, . . . [but] more importantly, greater responsibility for the ultimate output of the organization."

3. A "less authoritarian work culture . . . [which would] enable workers to be self-managers who are responsible for their own performance . . . with responsibility for scheduling work, ordering materials, hiring workers and the like [while] the foreman is replaced by a team leader. . . ."

4. That "workers, through their unions, are entitled to a decision-making role at all levels of the enterprise . . . [including]

strategic decisions . . . for example, . . . what new technologies should be acquired or about what changes to make in products or services."

5. That "the rewards realized from transforming the work organization to be distributed on equitable terms agreed upon through negotiations between labor and management . . . [which could] be achieved through increases in base wages or, in other cases, through agreements providing for some form of supplementary contingent compensation (such as gain sharing, profit sharing, stock ownership or the like) [and] is the product of a negotiated agreement between the employer and the union representing the workers." (AFL-CIO 1994, pp. 11–12)

Implicitly, the Federation's comments actually acknowledge the efficiency of employee participation. Its real objection to employee participation plans is its view that they are barriers to unionization. Organized labor regards employee participation as a device to circumvent the unfair employer practices of employer domination or interference with self-organization banned by the National Labor Relations Act. The general counsel of the AFL-CIO, in testimony opposing the proposed TEAM act, said in 1997:

> The "involvement" that the proponents of this bill seek is the subjection of employees to management-created and management-controlled processes that create the form—but not the substance—of joint decision-making. (Bureau of National Affairs 1997a).

Some academics have attacked employee participation programs because unions encounter them in organizing drives, and have lost more representation elections when these plans were present than when they were not (Rundle, cited by LeRoy 1997, p. 7). The association of organization efforts and successes may indeed be linked to the presence of employee participation plans. As LeRoy observed, ". . . lawful teams may limit the potential for union organizing simply by improving dialogue between management and non-supervisory workers." (LeRoy 1997, p. 29). However, the association of employee participation with failures in organizing may illustrate the logical fallacy, *post hoc, ergo propter hoc:* after this, therefore because of this. Unionization was already declining when employee participation was in its infancy, and if it is not as widespread as the AFL-CIO and others report, then its negative impact, if any, has to be small.

Irrespective of their legality and in deterring unionization, the communication role of employee participation remains as follows:

1. Employers still may communicate directly with their employees, together or in groups, about wages, hours and working conditions or anything else as long as no unlawful threats or promises are made as provided in Section 8(c) of the act.

2. Employers may create, and even dominate and deal with employee committees, on subjects other than wages, hours, working conditions or other terms or conditions of employment—for example, efficiency, marketing or production. In fact, in *Electromation* specifically did not condemn employee committees designed as communication devices to promote general interests in quality and efficiency.

3. "Brainstorming" to gather information from employees is lawful because it does not include "bilateral mechanisms," as the board put it.

4. Committees may consist of employees and supervisors that perform management or adjudicative functions without "dealing with" management.

5. Committees of employees that are not dominated or assisted are lawful even if they are representative and utilize managers as facilitators, unless they are used to bypass the union in a unionized setting.

6. Suggestion boxes are lawful, at least for proposals by individuals.

7. Otherwise, lawful employee groups do not become unlawful just because employment terms are mentioned infrequently. (Irving 1994, p. 6)

Summing up the communications feature that remained after the board's decisions in *Electromation* and *Dupont*, that lawyer pointed out, ". . . there is wide latitude for employers wishing to communicate with their employees to do so without running afoul of *Electromation* or *Dupont* or any of the diverse 'key' tests of past, present, or future Board members" (Irving 1994, p. 9).

Eight

The Organized and Individual Systems in the New Millennium

What are the prospects for the individual and organized systems of labor relations on the eve of the next millennium? For the organized system, the question is, can unions make a comeback? If the answer to that question is no, it does not *ipso facto* assure the future of its competitive rival, the individual system of representation. A declining organized system adds to the opportunity for the individual system, but does not assure it. The individual system requires the demand of workers, as well as a management that actively (and legally) supports it (Chapter 1). In the absence of either, personnel and human resource management would determine employee relations, and these do not constitute the individual system of representation described in this book.

Three theorems offer insights into the possible future of the organized system: the "spurt," the "stagnation," and my own "twilight zone" theorem. The spurt theory argues that the expansion of the organized system has historically come episodically, rather than in a steady trend (Freeman 1986, p. 44). Three historical examples can illustrate the spurt theory. The first was the rapid expansion of unions affiliated with the American Federation of Labor, as well as unions independent of the Federation, in the early part of the twentieth century. Essentially, that spurt was largely the product of the economic power of unions in the construction and railway transportation industries. Except for World War I and a brief period after the war, unions made gains through their ability to exercise what economists identify as the need for their services (the relative inelasticity of demand for their labor) and their ability in some industries, like construction, to limit the supply of labor. The unions of the day often referred to it as a philosophy of "self-help" (Troy 1999).

The second episode illustrating the spurt theory was the formation and rapid growth of the CIO in the 1930s. That episode was assisted by the enactment of the National Labor Relations Act of 1935, which changed the dynamics of union growth in the private labor market. As described previously, however, the power of the law was largely dissipated in the 1950s as a result of the emergence of the service-dominated labor market and later by the New Age of Adam Smith (Chapter 3). The ability of new law to promote a new surge in unionism is unlikely, as indicated by the experience of Canada.

The third example of the surge theorem was the development and rapid expansion of unionism in the public labor market over the past four decades. Like private unionism after the enactment of the National Labor Relations Act in the 1930s, this episode was also associated with a radical change in public policy. Prior to President Kennedy's Executive Order 10988, issued in 1962, public policy alternated between benign neglect and hostility toward the unionization of government employees. President Roosevelt was opposed to the unionization of federal workers, although it had been tolerated for many years, primarily in the Postal Service, because of legislation early in this century. Before President Kennedy's order, New York City and the State of Wisconsin had adopted policies favorable to the unionization of their workers, but they were exceptions. After President Kennedy's order, numerous states began adopting legislation fostering unionism and bargaining. Very quickly, the change in public policy brought about a rapid growth of public unionism. The New Unionism reached higher density rates than were ever achieved by the private sector. However, the stimulus gradually weakened in the 1990s, and membership and density began to wane. In 1998 it rose again, but slightly. Unlike the private economy, where competitive forces eroded the organized system, government cutbacks in the Defense Department, the largest employer of civilian federal employees, slowdowns in government social initiatives, and attrition and turnover of membership have produced stagnation in the organized public sector. In any event, the surge episode in the public labor market has no relation to any potential in the private labor market because the factors governing unionism differ in the two markets.

As this book was nearing completion, a union win among home-care workers in Los Angeles County was reported by the media as the largest and most significant since the successful sit-down strike of the United Auto Workers (UAW) in the 1930s against General Motors (Greenhouse 1999). More than 70,000 home-care workers who served more than 200,000 seniors and disabled individuals were involved. The media's reports appeared to contradict my theory of the twilight zone governing the decline of the private organized system, or that there was a renewal of the surge theorem, as just described. The reports erred in numerous and important ways, however, and therefore did not challenge the twilight zone thesis or constitute a new episode in the surge theorem of union behavior. Among the most egregious errors in those reports was the implication that the union victory was in the private service sector. That was flatly wrong. It came in public services, a sector with extensive unionization, so there was no breakthrough in that industrial sector. Unreported were the roots of that the victory. About 1997, the Los Angeles County Board of Supervisors created a de facto single employer and a corresponding bargaining unit that enabled the union (the Service Employees International Union) to win the ensuing election easily, after a decade of unsuccessful efforts to organize the same employees. Hitherto, the county had dealt with its home-care workers on an individual basis, and all attempts to organize home-care workers had failed. The County Board of Supervisors changed its relationship with its home care workers about 1997 when it established a new public agency, the Personal Assistance Services Council, instead of the county itself, to be the employer (Bureau of National Affairs 1999). In one stroke, the county centralized the employer-employee relationship with its home-care workers and at the same time set up what would become the bargaining unit covering 70,000 workers. The union, seeing the welcome mat laid out, petitioned for the right to represent the "new" employees of the new county agency; not surprisingly, it easily won the right to represent them. Public-sector unions' win rates in representation elections with public employers average about 80 percent, if not higher, in contrast to 50 percent in the private labor market (Appendix Table 3). For a little more than a decade before the creation of the council, the union had been unsuccessful in its attempts to organize home-care workers. As the employer of record for the thousands of county home-care workers, the new council was also authorized to bargain with the union after it won the representation election. However, that was not all the County of Los Angeles did to ensure union representation of its home care employees; the county added clients and health-care activists to the council, putting the demanders in the unique position of being able to shape the quantity and quality of the care to be provided! One other point should be made: home-care workers' are unskilled, are low paid, and have a high turnover, and such workers have never been at the heart of the union movement. In contrast, the auto workers with whom the media compared them included very highly paid, skilled workers with low turnover. As manufacturing workers, they became the backbone of the private organized system. Finally, even as the misleading comparisons were being made by the media, the organized system's share of the private labor market sank to yet another new low, consistent with my theory of the twilight zone! (Appendix Figure 1).

Looking ahead to the new millennium, is another episode of the spurt theory possible for the private-sector labor movement? A new spurt by its nature is unpredictable. An egregious example of a miscalculation of a spurt in unionism was the prediction by the president of the American Economic Association on the eve of the New Deal that organized labor was "finished" as a major social and economic force in this country. Hardly had he spoken when history completely contradicted his forecast. Under the auspices of the New Deal, there was a record expansion of unions into companies, industries, and groups of workers hitherto impervious to unionization, most notably in the manufacturing sector. One must consider the possibility of a repetition of the 1930s, that a new spurt in unionism may be in the offing, given the size of its membership (9.3

million) and its current financial and political strength, compared to its capacities on the eve of the New Deal. Moreover, one must also consider the possibility of new labor laws in the new century that would reinvigorate private unionism. Nevertheless I discount the possibility of a resurgence of the private system of organized representation.

The second theory on union trends, the stagnation theorem, applies separately to the two measures that reflect union performance, density, and membership. The stagnation theory held that the market share of the private organized system had reached a plateau after World War II and would not expand any further. In fact, had it not been for the Korean War, the market penetration of the organized system would have been reached about 1948, instead of 1953. After its historic peak in 1953, the market share of the private-sector organized system has fallen annually without interruption to the present day.

In terms of the population of union members, the theory of stagnation appeared to have been breached after the Korean War when, in the 1960s, private sector union membership increased until topping out at an all-time high of 17 million in 1970. However, the war in Vietnam, even though it did not put the economy on a full-time war footing, did stimulate unionism in the goods industries, as war has always done, and postponed the long-run ebbing membership. After 1970, the organized system went from stagnation to decline, as private-sector membership (and market share) began to shrink regularly and drastically. Throughout the past three decades, the private organized system gave up nearly 8 million members. Therefore, by both major yardsticks of trends—membership and market share—the private organized system moved from stagnation into a state of decline, a decline I regard as irreversible.

This assessment is the basis of my theory on the future dynamics of the organized system, the theory of the "twilight zone" (Troy 1997). The theory argues that the private organized system in this country entered the twilight zone in the closing years of the twentieth century and will govern its trends into the new millennium; the other G-7 countries lag the United States, but the same theory applies to them. By twilight zone, I mean three things: First, a markedly reduced role for collective bargaining in the private economy of the United States and its restriction to a few key industries. Second, that the private sector organized system will probably enter the twenty-first century with almost the same market share it had at the beginning of the twentieth century. At that time it was 7 percent of private nonfarm employment, and at the turn of the new century, I expect it to be 9 percent. Third, with the onset of the new millennium, both systems are approaching their limits: limited further increase of the individual system and limited further decline of the organized system.

The Twilight Zone in the New Millennium

In contrast to the beginning of the twentieth century, the individual and organized systems begin the twenty-first century competing in many of the same major labor markets. Manufacturing is of particular importance. Currently, many of the most successful nonunion companies are located in the environs of the highest union densities as well as in vicinities of low union penetration. Geographically, the individual system is larger in every state and is growing most rapidly in states where employment is also expected to increase most in the next century. This is significant because it will ensure the continuing dominance of the individual system in the future.

Economic and technological changes have fostered the growing competitive advantage of the individual system by shifting output from traditional industries (steel and autos, for example) into high-tech goods. While autos and steel remain extensively unionized, the new high-tech manufacturing industries are not. Even in the centers of the organized system, the unions' advantage is waning. In autos, unions confront unorganized Japanese and German transplants, and a continuing flow of imports, and the innovative production system of modular construction. In steel production, the rise of nonunion minimills and foreign competition plays a similar role. Technological changes have altered the historic composition of employment in manufacturing and other goods industries, enhancing the advantage of the individual system. Far more white-collar workers are employed in manufacturing than in the past, and they constitute a pool of personnel inclined toward individual representation in the midst of the organized system. This occupational group will continue to expand within manufacturing (and in other industries), further shrinking the organized system's historical base, the blue-collar worker. In the largest labor market of the private economy, services, the organized systems' historical disadvantage will increase even more. High-tech services rely on professionals and managers, occupations that have historically held aloof from joining unions, and these are the occupations expected to grow the most as the economy moves into the next century.

The competitive positions of the two systems have been altered in ways other than changes in industries, in occupations, and in technology, and these, too, increase the competitive advantage of the individual system. While the individual system has undergone decades of competition with the organized model and has learned from it, the organized system appears to lag in developing new ideas and strategies, especially those needed to regain the initiative. John Dunlop, a friend of the organized system, observed that "American labor organizations . . . are shaped more basically by events of the past century than by the forces of the last fifteen years" (Dunlop 1978, p. 79). The election of John J. Sweeney to the presidency of the AFL-CIO in 1995 was greeted by announcements that a new leadership had new ideas that would reverse the organized system's continuing decline. On the television program *Think Tank*, one of the participants, Barry Bluestone, a well-known supporter of organized labor, after agreeing that unions were still relying on strategies of the past and with little success, opined that the new leadership of the AFL-CIO had new ideas that would reverse the long term decline of the organized system (Public Broadcasting System, *Think Tank* 1995). In response, the late Albert Shanker, president of the American Federation of Teachers and a member of the Executive Council of the AFL-CIO until he passed away said, ". . . as a member of the Executive Council [of the AFL-CIO], for 5, 10, 15 years, if they had a new idea, I would have heard it" (Public Broadcasting System, *Think Thank* 1995). The author, who also was a panelist, initiated that exchange by asking Bluestone to identify the AFL-CIO's new ideas, and it was this remark which elicited Mr. Shanker's rejoinder.

A new strategy which had been announced by Richard Trumka, the new number two man (Secretary-Treasurer) of the AFL-CIO, had warned employers in a public statement that they faced "business's worst nightmare" if they resisted the unionization of their employees (Public Broadcasting System 1995). The host of the program, Ben Wattenberg, queried the wisdom of the new management of the Federation to talk about creating a "nightmare" for American business. Bluestone agreed that he did not think it was wise, but that Secretary-Treasurer Trumka's idea was taken out of context and that he was referring only to firms that ran roughshod over labor and would now face a new and strengthened labor movement. Perhaps Bluestone meant that the unions would leverage pension funds to influence corporations through shareholder advocacy, corporate accountability issues, and development of global strategies for organizing and bargaining, but that was not clear.

Inasmuch as the Federation itself engages in virtually no new organization, a task reserved to its affiliated unions, and because, as president of the United Mine Workers of America, Trumka presided over the shrinkage of the union to a near vanishing point (it is currently discussing a merger with another union), employers have apparently taken his threat as more rhetoric than reality. Moreover, since his involvement in the fraudulent election of a former Teamster president, Ron Carey, which may yet lead to his indictment, Trumka's effectiveness as the spearhead of the resurgence of the organized system has been blunted.

In 1996, the AFL-CIO also announced additional measures to stimulate organizing, beginning with a program to restructure the personnel and finances of affiliated unions. A committee was set up, chaired by Arthur Coia, president of the Laborers' International Union of North America (Bureau of National Affairs, August 8, 1996). The choice was strange, inasmuch as the press had identified Coia as an associate of the Mafia. Other steps to energize union organizing soon followed. Six months after his election to the presidency of the AFL-CIO, John J. Sweeney announced to a conference sponsored jointly by the AFL-CIO and Cornell University that unions needed new strategies and tactics. Among the steps he proposed was a sharp increase in spending to organize, up to one-third of the Federation's budget to be spent on organizing. Certainly, the union movement is not short of the financial means for organizing. As of 1995, organized labor in the private sector owned assets in excess of $9.4 billion and took in revenues of $12.2 billion (Masters and Atkin 1997, Table 1). In addition, in 1995 the AFL-CIO signed an agreement with Household International, a major financial corporation, under which Household would pay $375 million to the Federation over a five-year period in exchange for the right to issue an AFL-CIO emblazoned credit card. Hence, money would not appear to be a problem for organizing in the future. Sweeney's approach to spending more on organizing recalls the vigorous and successful efforts of the late John L. Lewis, when he led the nascent committee, later the Congress of Industrial Organizations, in the 1930s. Sweeney's proposals could be described as human resource management from the unions' perspective. At the same time, Sweeney also pointed out that simply spending more money will not be enough, and that more organization should be done without resorting to the procedures of the National Labor Relations Act. He invited university professors to "brainstorm" the necessary research about workers and employers that would assist unions to organize. Apropos of that, staff members of unions and faculty from Cornell and the University of Minnesota presented analyses dealing with overcoming employer opposition, organizing women and low-wage workers, and workers' attitudes about unions and organizing. One union leader pointed out that unions needed to organize 300,000 members a year to maintain the current percentage of union members, and 1 million additional members to increase its market share by 1 percent. As difficult as the short-term outlook may be, the long-term outlook is far worse. I have calculated that the unions would need 25 million new private-sector members—while holding on to all 9.3 million they now enroll, or a total membership of more than 35 million members—to regain their 1953 peak market share of 36 percent. To regain the peak membership population of 17 million of 1970 also is a hopeless task. To paraphrase a familiar saying, "It's the numbers, stupid."

One proposed organizing strategy would require unions to forgo their jurisdictional claims occasionally. A number of private sector unions have already done so, organizing or acquiring through merger groups of public employee unions. Whether the affected public employee unions (also affiliates of the AFL-CIO) approve is doubtful, given the history of jurisdictional battles unions have waged with one another. Another recommendation to increase the success rate in organizing was to enlarge the scope of organizing to blanket an industry or community. Unions were also advised that organizing must go beyond the old tactics and embrace political action and community relations (Bureau of National Affairs 1996).

A similar and later conclave of the AFL-CIO and university faculty in California recommended that unions concentrate on the quality of potential new members, not on the "hard numbers." This was proposed by an academic in an address to activists and leaders from various labor and community organizations, as well as students and professors during a "teach-in" titled "Fighting for Social Justice," part of a week-long meeting of the Executive Council of the AFL-CIO in Los Angeles (Bureau of National Affairs 1997a). Earlier, in 1996, Sweeney and other labor leaders announced plans to organize strawberry workers and apple pickers, groups similar to Sweeney's "Justice for Janitors" organizational campaigns of previous years. The Federation established a fund, to reach $20 million, aimed at organizing 30,000 strawberry and apple pickers, at a cost of about $670 per worker. So far, this purported and expensive campaign has made little headway, and little has been said about it either in the media or by the AFL-CIO. Historically, the organized system never regarded such low-skilled workers as important to the cause and core of unionism. In fact, the historical meaning of the term *trade union* clearly indicates that the origins and development of organized labor depended on the skilled (trade) occupations. Only with the rise of the Congress of Industrial Organizations did unions enroll unskilled workers on a large scale, and this was a by-product of organizing on an industrial basis. Another exception are the unionized unskilled laborers in the construction industry, a development made feasible only because they were associated with the extensive unionization of skilled workers in the industry. In general, unskilled laborers, particularly in agriculture, are difficult to organize because of their high employment turnover as well as the limited skills required by their jobs, making their replacement readily available.

While the foregoing relates to organizing the unorganized, the Federation also turned to methods of halting the decline of the existing union movement. The principal step in this campaign was industrial policy—opposition to "fast-track" authority for the president in negotiating future trade agreements. The AFL-CIO correctly attributed much of the loss in unionism to international trade. Organized labor was successful in its opposition; nevertheless, union ranks continued to thin, as reported in the latest statistics of the Bureau of Labor Statistics (BLS). Private-sector membership in nonfarm industries declined by 47,000, and union market share fell .2 points to 9.6 percent of employment in 1997–1998. Likewise, measured by representation elections in previously unorganized units conducted by the National Labor Relations Board (NLRB), not only have the new strategies and ideas failed to reverse the downward momentum of the organized system, they confirm the continuing ebb of the organized system.

In another strategy to counter the impact of the migration of nonunion jobs and production into the United States, the leadership of the AFL-CIO considered engaging in cross-country unionization. For example, they proposed that the Metalworkers Federation in Germany help the United Auto Workers organize the runaway BMW plant in South Carolina and the Mercedes plant in Georgia (Public Broadcasting System 1995). To date, both factories remain nonunion. Now that Chrysler and Mercedes have merged, speculation centers on what, if anything, the senior partner, Mercedes, will do, to facilitate the unionization of its plant in Georgia. Will it accept unionization as it apparently does in Germany, and as Chrysler does in the United States? I doubt that the company will. In Germany, postwar policies, especially those of the British during the Occupation, initiated unions and works' councils in basic German industries, and German governments that followed built on these early beginnings. German companies that have migrated to the United States seem anxious to avoid the union arrangements they have in Germany.

On the export side of the unions' problem, many firms are outsourcing and setting up operations overseas, presenting organized labor with "serious challenges in job flight" (Bureau of National Affairs 1997a). In a thus far futile attempt, AFL-CIO President John Sweeney traveled abroad to build ties with unions in other countries in order to encourage them to organize the employees of companies fleeing America in hopes of stemming the loss of jobs in the United States. No evidence exists of any measurable success from his endeavors. Finally, the Teamsters's strike against the United Parcel Service (UPS) and its settlement was acclaimed as breathing new life into the claim that organized labor in the private economy was now coming back. Obviously it did not.

Would New Labor Law Avert the Twilight Zone?

Thus far, organized labor's new strategies to organize the unorganized have been unsuccessful in turning around the organized system. Could new labor law that is more supportive of the organized system accomplish that goal and avert the twilight zone? In a word, I answer no. The evidence for my judgment is the declining private union movement of Canada. Despite legal protections patterned after the National Labor Relations Act, but far more protective of the organized system than in the United States, the Canadian private union movement has nevertheless been declining for about the past quarter century. Quebec, which has the most labor protectionist labor policies of any political jurisdiction north of the Rio Grande has, like the rest of Canada, also experienced decline.

Before these facts were demonstrated (Troy 1999), the AFL-CIO and many sympathetic scholars urged the revision of American labor relations policies based on Canadian models. Their belief that Canada had escaped the "American disease" of union decline rested on incorrect comparisons between Canadian and American labor markets and union data. Essentially, they compared noncomparable employment and noncomparable union statistics. Those comparisons were based on data that included both the public and the private sectors, while the composition of employment and union membership differs widely between the two countries.

This made comparisons one of apples to oranges: in the United States, union membership is (still) predominantly private, whereas in Canada it is overwhelmingly public. The same shortcoming applies to Canadian employment statistics, that is, the public sector in Canada is far larger, measured in relative terms, than the American. Because public-sector unionism is not subject to the competitive forces applicable to private unionism, any comparison that includes both union groups obscures what is going on in the private labor market. Although separate data for the two sectors, both in membership and employment, have been historically available for the United States, such is not the case for Canadian statistics. As a result, the official Canadian statistics until recently, although not comparable to the American statistics, have clearly registered decline (Troy 1999).

Even after these facts became generally recognized, the AFL-CIO and many academics continued to urge new labor law for the United States, based on the Canadian model, as the remedy for reviving the private organized sector in this country. The starting point for that policy was a landmark article in the *Harvard Law Review* in 1983 that described the National Labor Relations Act as an "elegant tombstone for a dying institution" (Weiler 1983, p. 1769). Weiler charged that "protracted" employer campaigns against organizing the unorganized "create a setting that elicits employer coercion of . . . employee choice . . . [which] the current system of unfair labor practice remedies has proved powerless to contain . . . or to undo" (Weiler 1983, pp. 1769–1770). Others said employer opposition was slowly strangling the organized system in the private economy (Freeman and Medoff 1984).

The arguments against employer behavior and the board's inability to deal with it not only became the conventional explanation for the decline of the organized system from the 1980s into the present time, it also led the Clinton administration to establish a special commission to reexamine the nation's labor law and its administration in 1993. That body was known officially as the Commission on the Future of Worker-Management Relations (hereafter, "the Commission"). It was popularly known as the Dunlop Commission after its chairman, retired Harvard professor John T.

Dunlop. The Commission began its work in the spring of 1993 and ended it in December 1994. In contrast to the Carter administration in 1977, when it faced the same problem of legislating a reversal of declining unionism in its proposed labor reform act, the Clinton administration created a select panel of nominally disinterested experts to propose legislative recommendations. However, the panel was not balanced as claimed by Labor Secretary Robert Reich; a majority were prounion. This outcome reflected the stated attitude of then Secretary Reich. In an address to the 1993 AFL-CIO convention, he told the Federation convention that the Clinton administration identified itself completely with the interests of organized labor, that "our agendas are exactly the same."

Officially, the Commission was given three tasks:

1. What (if any) new methods or institutions should be encouraged, or required, to enhance workplace productivity through labor-management cooperation and employee participation?

2. What (if any) changes should be made in the present legal framework and practices of collective bargaining to enhance cooperative behavior, improve productivity, and reduce conflict and delay?

3. What (if anything) should be done to increase the extent to which workplace problems are directly resolved by the parties themselves, rather than through recourse to state and federal courts and government regulatory bodies?

In sum, the Commission's central task was to examine and report on contemporary labor relations and recommend labor policies that looked to the new millennium. In my judgment, the Commission's recommended reforms of the American workplace, with one notable exception, looked backward to the 1930s and 1940s, an era when the visible hand of government was conspicuous in labor markets, and not toward the twenty-first century, an era more likely to depend on the invisible hand of worldwide competition. In my judgment, the Commission's only look to the future was its recommendation for legislation that would legalize employee participation programs in the nonunion labor market (Chapter 7). Except for the employee participation programs, the Commission's only other consideration of nonunion workers in the private economy was the possibility that they might join unions based on the Freeman-Rogers's surveys (Chapter 7). Commission recommendations focused primarily on how to revive the organized system of labor relations in the next century, and in that sense, it was looking to the past, rather than the future.

The Commission's majority approval of employee participation programs created a controversy within the Commission, the only one of its recommendations that led to dissent. The Commission's findings of fact on employee participation programs demonstrated their value in enhancing productivity, a fact of special importance in an increasingly competitive world, as the Commission's majority recognized. However, it faced the steadfast opposition of organized labor in approving employee participation in nonunion workplaces. In an attempt to overcome the objections of organized labor, the Commission proposed language reaffirming workers' general right to organize, the right of supervisors and other managerial personnel who participate in employee participation programs to join unions, and finally, language reinforcing the existing ban on employer-dominated labor organizations, which unions consider employee participation programs to be (Chapter 7). When the Commission recommended extending the right of supervisors to organize, it not only was looking backward but was trying to provide an avenue for the unionization of managerial participants of employee participation programs, supervisors in general, and to facilitate the unionization of production workers.

Except for its approval of employee participation and its interest in the potential demand of nonunion workers for organized representation, the Commission did not comment on the rights of workers who do not belong to unions, although the right not to be a union member has been part of the National Labor Relations Act since 1947, in the absence of a union shop agreement and in states with laws banning such agreements (right-to-work laws). In a follow-up of the Commission's report, one of its members noted that those participating in employee participation programs should have the right to draw on the "expertise" of outside organizations—unions and professional associations, for assistance. This, he pointed out, would enable unions to become "full service agents" to workers by providing them with information on enforcing their legal rights, promoting self-governance at the workplace, and consultation and technical services on safety and health, new work systems, education, training, labor market information, and other issues. He also attached collective bargaining representation as another resource workers could turn to and which unions could offer as "full service agents" (Kochan 1995). As Michael LeRoy learned from his study of employee participation groups, they already do exchange information with similar teams and groups, although the practice is not widespread (LeRoy 1997). None of the exchanges LeRoy reported involved unions or professional associations (which are unions by another name) or union-management cooperation teams. For nonunion management to agree to consult with unions or unionized labor-management teams would be tantamount to inviting the fox to visit the chicken coop. On the other hand, some unions would also oppose such consultation because cooperation with nonunion employee participation groups, they believe, would only strengthen the individual system of representation.

Given the composition of the Commission, it was not surprising that it identified employer opposition as a major factor in the decline of the organized system. In its commentary, however, it did not distinguish between the loss of union membership caused by the downsizing of the organized system (the disappearance of bargaining units) from the unions' unsuccessful efforts to organize the unorganized. The organized system's loss arising from downsizing is the major reason for the shrinkage of membership over the past three decades, and it has little, if any, relationship to employer opposition. The disappearance of bargaining units and its attendant loss of membership and decline in union organization are the result of structural changes in the economy—the shift from a goods-dominated to a service-dominated labor market—and its corollary, the downsizing of business, mergers, plant removal, and companies going out of business (Chapter 2). The Commission also ignored the difference between legal and illegal employer opposition in organizing drives. Even the harshest critic of employer behavior, Paul Weiler, who was counsel to the Commission, acknowledged the distinction. Previous to his service with the Commission, he wrote: "Most employers still do fight within the legal rules of the contest" (Weiler 1988, p. 7).

This distinction did not appear in the Commission's report, although Weiler was counsel to the Commission.

Apropos of employers' illegal actions that thwarted unions' organizing campaigns, the Commission called attention to the large number of illegal discriminatory discharges under section 8(a)(3) of the act, which bans such employer behavior. What the Commission did not explain was that many of the violations under that section of the law are the result of illegal employer actions unrelated to discouraging organizational campaigns. Among them are transfers and demotions unconnected to organizing; the reduction of an employee's seniority at the request of the union because of delinquency in dues payment; or discharge of an employee at the request of the union because the employer, complying with the requirement under a union shop agreement, discharges a worker for illegal reasons. In sum, a large number of illegal employer actions are unrelated to a union's organizing campaign but are classified under the same section of the law, distinctions that the Commission did not note in its reports. Consequently, many board-ordered reinstatements under 8(a)(3) were not for illegal discharges for union activity but for other reasons (LaLonde and Meltzer 1991). On the other hand, the general counsel of the AFL-CIO claimed that illegal employer actions are understated because many go unreported (Bureau of National Affairs 1996). That may well be true, but in the absence of data such claims are difficult to evaluate.

The Commission's most important recommendation acknowledging the New Age of Adam Smith was, as already noted, its endorsement (with qualifications) of employee participation groups in the nonunion domain. Ironically, the Commission's general backward look parallels the direction in which unions are moving. If present trends continue, by the year 2000–2001, the private sector union movement will have slipped back a century. As already noted, when the new millennium begins, unions' share of private employment will likely fall to 9 percent, nearly the same proportion it was at the beginning of the twentieth century. Another look backward was the Commission's recommendation for card checks instead of representation elections to certify a bargaining representative (a procedure virtually abandoned by the NLRB in the aftermath of Taft-Hartley); it expedited representation elections, government intervention in first contract settlements, and union access to shopping malls during an organization. Many of these recommendations were borrowed from the Canadian model, despite the knowledge that these legal measures had failed to prevent or halt the decline of private unionism in Canada.

In the end, the Commission's recommendations came to naught when the Republicans won control of the House of Representatives in 1994. (They already had control of the Senate.) However, assuming that Congress, one or both Houses, reverts to the Democrats, and if the Democrats also control the presidency and adopt proposals encouraging the organized system, would this lead to the comeback of the organized system? Revisiting the question does not change the conclusion, and for the same reason: the experience of Canada.

In addition to the market forces that are steering the organized system into the twilight zone, unions have internal problems, for example, those of corruption, and these also presage no resurgence of the organized system in the new century. If it can be said that the success of unionization is a fairly direct function of the failure of management to discover and attend to employees' dissatisfaction, it can also be said that union leadership has failed to come to grips with the organized system's overriding problem: decline. Fifteen years ago, the AFL-CIO was advised by its consultants that, unless changes occur in addressing that issue,

> . . . more of the same is likely to lead to more of the same: losses of organizing elections, a shrinking of the trade union movement, and even ultimately a slow and agonizing demise. Up or down, there is a clear rejection of the notion of having a union by non-union workers of the country by better than 2 to 1. Trade unions have become remote, at best, an anathema at worst, to most non-union workers in this country by the mid-1980s. (Harris and Associates 1984, p. 2).

The malaise of the union movement was addressed by a committed unionist, a person who spent his lifetime as an organizer, an editor of numerous AFL-CIO publications, a pamphleteer and educator. Harry Keller found the union movement's credibility as a democratic institution in a questionable state. He pointed out that "at virtually every AFL-CIO convention, the election of the Executive Council's 33 vice-presidents takes place in a matter of minutes, about as much time as the introduction of a guest speaker" (Keller 1990, p. 6). Keller also called attention to the leadership's remoteness from the rank and file. He described *The AFL-CIO News* as a "dull, bloodless" newspaper, slanted in its reporting. He pointed out that the *News* ignored the major defeat of UAW at Nissan and offered no commentary on its significance. The *News* heralded union victories in organizing as presaging a new age, a characterization that was later repeated by union spokesmen (and the media) in the UPS strike, even though the facts pointed to a contrary conclusion. Keller also said that the *News* reported nothing about the consent agreement between the U.S. government and the Teamsters that set up a trusteeship to oversee the union's activities: "In the pages of the *News* unions don't lose elections, union leaders are never guilty of wrongdoing, and internal dissension in unions is simply nonexistent" (Keller 1990, p. 9). All this sounds like the jokes making the rounds in the old Soviet Union that there was no truth in *Pravda* (the meaning of the word), or any news in *Ivestia* (the meaning of the word).

Thus far, the new ideas and strategies promised from the new leadership of the AFL-CIO have come to naught, and nothing on the horizon suggests any turnaround. Even if these drawbacks were not present, market analysis suggests that there is little the union movement can do to rescue itself. The organized system is the victim of economic changes to which unions can respond only to a limited degree—programs of union-management cooperation, and opposition to expanded free trade.

Marxists attributed the organized systems' decline to a repudiation of working-class interests by the labor movement, rather than the opposition of capitalist employers:

> . . . although there is a great deal of evidence to suggest that a concerted capitalist offensive has been underway since the early 1970s against U.S. labor unions, there is little to indicate that it has greatly accelerated the decline in victory rates of unions in certification elections during this period [1972–1979]. (Goldfield 1982, p. 199)

The cause of the decline, according to Marxian analysis, was less a result of a concerted capitalist offensive and "more directly traced to major . . . defeats suffered by the working class, and the left wing within it, from the 1930s to the mid-1950s—the period, that is, just before the beginning of the steady decline" (Goldfield 1982, p. 203). The key defeats of the working class and the left wing were not inflicted by employers (the natural class enemy), but by the union movement itself. In 1949–1950, the CIO expelled eleven unions charged by the CIO of being dominated by communists and acting against the interests of workers. Accordingly, the labor movement lost its organizing fervor. Subsequently, most of the expelled unions either merged with other CIO or AFL unions or disappeared because they lacked the support of organized workers. It is also worthy of note that Walter Reuther, the president of the CIO at the time of the expulsions and leader of the campaign for their expulsion, was a social democrat.

The Individual System in the New Millennium

The individual system's long-run durability depends on the workers' demand for individual representation and legal managerial policies to sustain it. Workers' demand for representation is also a cornerstone of the organized system, but employers' opposition to unions is regularly cited as the principal obstacle to organizing the unorganized. While workers' demand is doubtless the most important factor for both systems, the role of employers is not symmetrical. Employers' legal support for the individual system is more important to that system than are employers' illegal actions opposing the organized system.

Workers' demand for the system can be measured in several ways. The surveys of nonunion workers' propensity to join unions are one measure. Until the 1990s, as noted in Chapter 4, these surveys consistently showed that about two-thirds of nonunion workers reported that in a secret ballot election they would not vote for a union. A survey of 1994 included in the final report of the Commission on the Future of Worker-Management Relations found that 55 percent of nonunion workers said they would not vote for a union,

32 percent would vote for, and 13 percent were undecided (Free-man and Rogers 1997). The Lipset/Meltz survey of 1996 reported that 45 percent of employed nonunion workers would vote for a union and (presumably) 55 percent would not. (Their findings did not provide figures on those who would not vote for a union or who were uncertain).

All these surveys are "static," that is, they constitute findings at a point in time. The need to conduct the survey over more than a single day does not alter its static character. Moreover, they only reflect workers' intentions, not their actual behavior. As previously noted, this is the equivalent of the concept of "demand" in economics. It states a wish, but until that wish is translated into "effective demand," whether for a product or for the services of a union, or for individual representation, the intent version of demand is only speculation about real worker behavior.

A dynamic record of nonunion workers' effective demand for the organized and the individual system is readily at hand in the statistics of the NLRB. By "dynamic" is meant what happens over time, in contrast to the point in time of the surveys. The board has been conducting secret ballot representation elections among unorganized groups of workers since its inception in 1935. Unions' requests for these elections are undertaken only when there is a substantial demonstration of interest by the unorganized workers. The minimum legal requirement for a union to petition the board for an election is 30 percent of the anticipated bargaining unit (the voting district), but unions rarely seek an election with a minimum showing of interest. Although the board does not maintain records of the showing of interest, anecdotal information indicates that the unions rely on a range from more than one-half to three-quarters of the proposed bargaining unit before petitioning the board for an election. In addition, unions will seek a bargaining unit (voting district) in which they can reasonably expect to win. Employers may contest the scope of the bargaining unit for opposite reasons. The ultimate authority in defining the proposed bargaining unit is the NLRB.

What makes the board's data on representation elections valuable is not only that they demonstrate what is happening over time but, and this is most important, they report actual worker response to the question, Would you vote for a union in your workplace in a secret ballot election? This or a similar question is typical of surveys, but only the board's data translate intentions into realities. Curiously, these data, as formulated here, have been neglected in the literature dealing with nonunion employees' demand for organized representation. Instead, studies reporting NLRB election results display the number of elections, the number of votes for and against unions, the number of workers eligible to vote, the identity of the winners and losers, and other information. Very often, secondary reports on NLRB elections also include elections other than those involving previously unorganized workers. In this report, I use only those elections involving unorganized workers. These statistics reveal what we seek: workers' demand for representation, organized or individual.

To measure that demand, I have combined the number of votes for no union (individual representation) in elections won and lost by the unions only in unorganized units, 1970–1997.

That combination constitutes the total number of votes for no union representation, that is, for individual representation, and therefore corresponds to the intent of the question, Do you want to be represented by a union or not? (The board shuns treating a vote for no union as equivalent to a vote for individual representation, but since there is no alternative option, a vote for no union is, indeed, a vote for individual representation, and is so presented here.)

The results of this method of classification are reported in Appendix Table 1 for the years 1970 to 1997. The year 1970 was chosen as the starting year because the organized system reached its all-time peak of 17 million members at that time, and the nearly three decades of data are more than adequate to demonstrate a trend.

Appendix Table 1 shows that the number of votes for no union (individual representation) in elections averaged more than 50 percent over the twenty-eight-year span. The figures suggest several observations and questions. First, the number of unorganized nonunion workers who rejected unionism (favored individual representation) in board elections fell substantially below the percentage reported by surveys. The surveys have averaged about two-thirds of unorganized workers as rejecting union representation, except in the Lipset-Meltz survey, which indicates that the rejection rate had dropped to 55 percent. The question is, why are the surveys' rates of rejection of organized representation so much higher than the actual rate? The gap is explained by several reasons. First, as previously noted, unions petition for elections and for units in which their prospects of winning are best. Therefore, the unions' "selected sample" from NLRB elections would account for part of the gap. Perhaps another explanation is that employer opposition is not as effective in defeating unions as is generally believed. Appendix Table 1 also indicates that workers' decisions about joining unions change over time. In the early 1970s, nonunion workers demand for unionization was greater until the recession began in 1974. From that time on, the demand for individual representation exceeded the demand for representation in each succeeding year, except 1983, 1984, and 1996. Appendix Table 1 also suggests that the political party in power apparently had little impact on the trend in workers' demand for individual or organized representation. This observation is doubtless in conflict with the conviction held by most academics, the public, and the media. The best showing for organized representation came under President Nixon, two more years during the Reagan administration, and one (1996) under Clinton. The highest rejection rates for the organized system came during the Reagan years. The years of the Clinton administration showed little deviations from a long term trend. Appendix Table 1 also shows that the number of workers voting in elections of the NLRB has declined sharply. Since 1980, there have been only five years in which the number of votes exceeded 100,000. This could indicate that unions were not actively engaged in efforts to organize, as John J. Sweeney contended when he sought and won the presidency of the AFL-CIO in 1995. It could also reflect a growing disenchantment with unions among the unorganized.

Another insight into this possibility are the results of decertification elections. As noted earlier in this book, the Taft-Hartley Act of 1947 made it possible for workers (not employers) to remove a union as their bargaining representative. Decertification elections are not as numerous as elections in previously unorganized units, and they are difficult to mount. They account for little more than 10 percent of organizing elections and involve fewer workers. Nevertheless, they offer a perspective on the question, do organized workers want a union to continue to represent them?

For the 1970–1997 period, Appendix Table 2 presents the total number of decertification elections held, who won, the total votes for nonunion (individual representation), and that number as a proportion of total votes cast. As in Appendix Table 1, I combined the votes for nonunion (individual representation) in elections that unions won and lost to measure the workers' demand to continue to be represented by a union.

Several conclusions emerge from the data in Appendix Table 2. First, the demand for nonunion (individual representation), measured by the number of elections, clearly establishes an overwhelming preference for nonunion representation. Throughout the nearly three decades of data, individual representation won nearly three-fourths of all elections. At the same time, individual representation won just over half the votes. This indicates that the demand for individual representation is strongest in small establishments. The majority vote is close to that of nonunion workers voting to choose or reject organized representation, as depicted in Appendix Table 1. This suggests that the same reasons underlie many workers' attitudes toward individual representation before and after a decision to support the organized system.

Appendix Table 3 reports the results of elections in units previously unorganized for the period 1970–1997. It shows the rate of success or failure to win units (disregarding votes) and is therefore yet another measure of unorganized workers' demand for organized or individual representation. Over the twenty-eight years in the table, only a little more than half of the weighted average were won by unions, but the organized and the individual systems split the total number of elections, (fourteen years each). The weighted average of elections for individual representation, 49.5 percent, shown in Appendix Table 3 closely approaches the total votes for individual representation, 50.1 percent (Appendix Table 1). The data of these tables reinforce my conclusions that the organized system is headed toward the twilight zone.

Management in the New Millennium

Next to a dramatic reversal of nonunion workers' current preference for individual representation, the greatest potential challenge to the individual system in the new century is a nonunion management lapsing into hubris. Given the trends toward individual representation, management overconfidence could sow the seeds of unionism. Neglect of workers' problems has long been recognized by management, and others, as fertile ground for organizing. One analyst who is "bearish" on the outlook for the future of the organized system observed that "as the 'threat effect' of unions continues to decline . . . some firms will inevitably fall into the trap of opportunism and insensitivity toward employees, and this would persuade workers that they needed a union" (Kaufman 1997, p. 483). Bread-and-butter issues remain important grounds for joining unions, but, as Appendix Table 1 demonstrates, there is no evidence of a rising support for unions.

Philosophically, the problem of managing in the nonunion system of industrial relations is constancy of purpose. Constancy requires investment of more managerial time in the individual than in an organized model (Chapter 5). While it takes considerably more time and care in dealing with employees in a nonunion environment, it also provides management with the opportunity to be more flexible than would be likely under a union contract. On the other hand, there are occasions when company rules and policies may be more cumbersome than the terms of a union contract because supervisory and middle management are wary of potentially being overruled by higher management's commitment to the individual system. This strains the integrity of the individual system's grievance procedure, one of the system's sources of durability.

Although neglect of real issues occurs periodically, it is likely to be infrequent because managerial personnel have been vetted by the experiences of the past, especially the experience of the 1920s and 1930s. They have also been vetted by experience with labor law particularly under the amended National Labor Relations Act (the 1947 Taft-Hartley Act). These legal changes facilitated employers' ability to oppose unions legally. There are many legal actions an employer may now take when a union attempts to organize its workers. For example, management may inform employees that while the union is free to promise them anything, changes in actual conditions of employment must await negotiations and an agreement. Management may also tell employees of the benefits they currently have, compare them and all other terms and conditions of employment with other companies in the area, unionized or not. They may also furnish employees with information on the pay they would lose in strikes of various durations, the level of any strike benefits the union provides, and the amount of union dues. Employers are legally within their rights to keep nonemployee organizers off the company premises. Within the context of the multiple legal "do's and don'ts," managerial campaigns to remain nonunion play defense as well as offense. Management tries to anticipate what the union may do by reviewing past as well as current union campaign strategies and tactics. Since employers may legally listen to what employees have to say about the union, the feedback becomes a vital input in their tactics. They can review the union's history and background in both the local area and nationally. If the union has attempted to organize other companies in the area, management may contact them about the union's campaign and its effectiveness, as well as the company's actions. Management may review the union's strike history, local and national, and collect relevant newspaper articles and pictures about that history. Other management steps are to obtain and review copies of the union's contracts with local companies, review the international union's constitution and the bylaws of the local, and obtain copies of the union's financial reports filed with the U.S. Department of Labor. These are open to the public. A master list of backup material from this "data bank" can be prepared for supervisors for use during the organizing campaign.

Before leaving the subject of employer opposition to union organizing, it should be noted that opposition to the organization of the unorganized is not exclusive to private enterprise. Unions have more than once been declared in violation of the National Labor Relations Act in their role as employers when their own employees attempted to organize a union to represent them. Although generally unfamiliar to the public and typically ignored in the literature associating employer opposition only to businesses, it is well-settled legal doctrine that when a labor organization takes on the role of an employer, the act applies to its operations just as it would to any other employer (U.S. National Labor Relations Board, 250 NLRB 880). In one case, the litany of the union's illegal actions included discharge, discriminatory transfers motivated by reprisal, surveillance, threatening employees with reprisals for filing charges with the board, suspending employees because of their organizing activities, refusal to bargain collectively through representatives of their own choosing, reassigning job duties in order to retaliate for employees' legally protected activities, and discouraging membership in their union. As with any employer found in violation of the act, the board ordered the union defendant to take steps to rectify its wrongdoing: offer full reinstatement of illegally discharged employees to their former jobs or, if those jobs no longer exist, to substantially equivalent jobs, without prejudice to seniority or other rights and privileges, and make them whole for any loss of pay suffered by reason of their discharge, with interest; bargain collectively with the union of its employees with respect to wages, hours, and other terms and conditions of employment; post at its facility copies of the board's order and maintain them for sixty consecutive days thereafter in conspicuous places, including all places where notices to employees are customarily posted, and take reasonable steps to ensure that the notices are not altered, defaced, or covered by any other material. I provide the foregoing detail in order to show that self-interest applies to employers generally, and although the extent of illegal activities of unions-as-employers is small, the principles and legal issues involved are general, not unique to for profit enterprises.

Why Most Nonunion Workers Will Continue to Prefer Individual Representation

The basic reason I believe most nonunion workers will prefer a non-union status in the future is the absence of a compelling incentive to join a union: "Simply put, the union route is an irrelevant way to solve their [nonunion workers'] problems" (Harris and Associates 1984, p. 29). That question, I believe, still holds true today. More recent attitudinal information reports that 59 percent of workers (perhaps including unionized as well) would prefer to solve workplace problems on their own (Lipset and Meltz 1996). The same survey reported 66 percent of nonunion employed workers would prefer not to belong to a union. The survey did not pursue the reasons for these results, whereas the Harris survey for the AFL-CIO did. In fact, the Harris survey remains the most comprehensive assessment of why nonunion workers refrain from joining.

Another insight into why nonunion workers can be expected to prefer the individual system in the future is suggested by Adam Smith's theory of compensating or equalizing differentials. An equalizing difference for the nonunion worker is his experience and preference for a workplace culture different from that under collective bargaining, despite the union's relative wage advantage. It should be recalled that part of the union wage advantage is explained by the discipline and impersonal work rules under a bargaining agreement. Verma, an academic friendly to the organized system commented that ". . . [nonunion] workers today have acquired a 'taste' for a cooperative, productive and an informal workplace. A workplace characterized by conflict, legalistic and impersonal work rules, and lack of concern for the economic health of the organization [company] is no longer attractive even with the lure of higher wages" (Verma 1983, p. 172). Unions, he also commented, rose to power in an era of conflict (the 1930s and 1940s), an era foreign to the outlook of the contemporary nonunion worker.

Not only are nonunion workers satisfied with their jobs, they see no need for a union to retain job satisfaction. The nonunion worker associates job satisfaction with the job, and therefore with the employer. And the more satisfied the worker, the more likely he will remain nonunion. Thus, one explanation for the decline of the organized system during the 1980s stated that it was "correlated with an increase in the satisfaction of nonunion workers with their jobs . . . [coupled with] a decline in nonunion workers' beliefs that unions are able to improve wages and working conditions" (Farber 1989, Abstract). Thus, the one issue that could attract nonunion workers—the bread-and-butter issue of better compensation—exerts less attraction than is commonly believed. As a nonunion worker at Nissan was quoted at the time of the representation election in July 1989: "They [the UAW] can't give us anything we don't already have" (*Newark Star-Ledger*, July 23, 1989, p. 3). On the other hand, union workers also associate job satisfaction with the union and, indeed, this was one of the strengths of the union movement. Essentially, then, the nonunion worker associates job satisfaction with the job and the employer, an attachment comparable to the union member who associates job satisfaction with the union and collective bargaining.

There are also specific issues, such as the cost of strikes and union dues, which nonunion workers find off-putting. More important, there is a gap between the nonunion worker and the union: "Put bluntly, unions have become remote, diffused in their reputation to those [nonunion] workers, and not really a part of their consciousness" (Harris and Associates 1984, p. 29). When nonunion workers were asked if they would join a voluntary association that offered a variety of services (such as unions offer), their interest was high until mention was made of affiliating the association with the AFL-CIO. Then, nonunion workers turned away from the association idea, just as they did when asked about their voting support for unions.

The class-struggle appeal of the 1930s and 1940s has given way to a new state of mind among workers, as many of whom regard themselves as middle class or aspire to that status for themselves and their children. The lower expectations of minorities in the labor market probably explain the continuing appeal of union representation to them. According to the Harris survey, it is only among minorities where class lines persist and "antipathy to employers is as much as it was in the 1930s" (Harris and Associates 1984, p. 27).

For most nonunion workers, the "we" versus "they" approach recalls more of the past than the present, and the individual system's philosophy builds on this change in attitudes. Conflicts of interest between employers and workers will necessarily persist, but the intensity of the conflicts has been dampened, as evidenced in the organized sector by the decline in strikes. Furthermore, instead of convergence between nonunion and union workers, as believed by some assessments (Harris and Associates 1984), I believe the two groups are growing apart in their outlook on how best to address and resolve the issues of workaday life. This gap increases as the organized system continues to decline. In such circumstances, nonunion workers must ask themselves if they should cast their lot with a labor movement that continues to fade.

To end on a philosophical note, the book began by citing the market as one of the principal mainstays of the individual system of representation. Adam Smith, the philosopher and prophet of the market system, put the individual at the center of his analysis of the economy, in contrast to the mercantilist school of thought of his time, whose focal point was government regulation of society and the economy. In this study, I have transferred that focus to labor relations.

———— Nine ————

Highlights and Summary

The most important and controversial finding of this study is the existence in the United States of a system of labor relations beyond unions and collective bargaining: the individual system of employee representation. I conclude that this is the result of a quiet revolution. It began nearly a half-century ago and now, on the eve of the new millennium, accounts for more than 90 percent and close to 90 million men and women of all employed workers in the private, nonfarm economy. Finally, the structural change in labor relations, the dominance of the individual over the organized system, is irrevocable.

The conditions requisite for the individual system consist of competitive markets for goods and services, technological changes, and changes in the structure of employment. Conversely, the same forces are responsible for the sag of the private organized system. The decline of the organized system opened employee representation to the potential of new concepts and practices that differed from nonunion labor relations prior to the New Deal. Central to the new concepts and practices are the demands of workers, as well as employers, for a system beyond unionism and bargaining. While employers' preference for a nonunion system can be taken as a given by virtue of experience, the demand of workers for individual representation had to be demonstrated as a necessary corollary. Empirically, it is demonstrated by surveys of workers' attitudes and, what is more important, by the statistical results of representation elections of unorganized workers conducted by the National Labor Relations Board (NLRB). It follows from these data that there is a model of the system of individual representation, just as there is for collective representation.

The observed behavior of unorganized workers is consistent with market theory, which underlies the model. The majority of non-union workers believe that the market can satisfy their needs and consequently prefer to vote for individual rather than organized representation. The fact that more than 90 percent of private-sector workers in the United States are outside the organized sector cannot be dismissed as a statistical artifact. On the contrary, it is a statistical demonstration of workers' participation rate in the non-union system.

The individual system dominates the historic industrial centers of the organized system—manufacturing, construction, mining, and transportation—as well as the labor market as a whole. This may surprise some who believe that these industries are still dominated by the organized system. Because most of these industries are also most affected by global competition, the individual system is better positioned to grow and compete successfully against the organized system in the highly competitive international economies of today and the new century.

To such questions as Who protects the interests of the individual worker? Who "negotiates" for him? this study responds that primarily it is the market. Although markets are imperfect, markets do function. Markets may be the worst form of allocating resources and rewarding people—except for all the others, to echo Winston Churchill's comment on democracy. In addition to markets, some institutions also protect the individual worker—including organized workers. Paradoxically, one of the most important protectors of the individual worker is the National Labor Relations Act. Even though the goal of the act has always been to encourage unionism and collective bargaining, even under its original and most prounion version, the Wagner Act of 1935, the National Labor Relations Act also recognized the right of employees not to choose a labor organization to represent them. In addition, other laws governing the workplace, employment laws, have legislated many rights and protections that affect the worker, organized or not. In fact, employment law (as distinct from labor relations law) has been identified by some analysts as a major cause for the decline of the organized system because it has become a substitute for many of the terms written into collective bargaining agreements.

Structural shifts in the nature of work, from making things to providing services, have profoundly affected both the individual and the organized systems. For the individual system, the shift has brought new opportunities to expand; for the organized system, the new service-dominated labor market has meant increased difficulties in organizing because it requires occupations and industries historically disconnected from the organized system's interests, including its ability to unionize. The structural transformation in the labor market, sometimes referred to as the postindustrial labor market, began in the mid-1950s in the United States. It was eventually emulated by all other major industrial nations, and with parallel consequences for their private-sector union groups. At the same time, the new labor market and increased competition domestically and internationally eroded the monopoly power of the National Labor Relations Act to prescribe the rules and conditions of organized labor relations and the organized system.

Another important conclusion of this study is that the New Deal created a great divide, a structural change in both the organized and nonunion systems of labor relations systems. Neither the individual nor the organized system since the New Deal era reprises the pre–New Deal era. While the original Wagner Act demolished the old nonunion system of industrial relations and left virtually nothing in its ruins, the Wagner Act also created a new organized system. Conditions began to change shortly after World War II. For nonunionism, the first development was the enactment of the Labor Management Relations Act (the Taft-Hartley Act) of 1947. The new law helped establish the individual system in several ways, but most important was its recognition of the right of workers *not to belong to unions, absent a union or agency shop agreement, and by enabling states to override these agreements with "right-to-work" laws.* The second development that gave rise to the contemporary individual system was the advent of the service-dominated labor markets in the mid-1950s. That change greatly facilitated the emergence and growth of the individual system because it reoriented the focus of the labor market from blue-collar occupations and industrial production to white-collar jobs, individualism in production, and a large array of new industries alien to the organized system. These institutional changes facilitated the rise of workers' demand for individual representation, accompanying the emergence of a new managerial class more sophisticated and knowledgeable in labor relations than their predecessors of the pre–New Deal era.

For the organized system, both developments—the Taft-Hartley Act and the emergence of the service labor market—were followed by a third development: global competition beginning in the 1970s. All three had severe adverse effects. Of the three, Taft-Hartley had at most only a marginal impact on the organized system, although it is often put in the forefront by unions and most academic specialists. The evidence that Taft-Hartley had only a marginal impact on the organized system is the experience of Canadian unions. Canadian unions, although operating under what is yet called Super Wagnerism, have wilted despite the protection of labor laws much more prounion than the Wagner Act ever was. Moreover, all other G-7 countries' private union movements have fallen, despite favorable legal climates. Far more damaging to the organized system than labor law in the years since World War II, was the rise of the service-dominated labor markets, which unions could not organize, and the growing power and sweep of competition at home and abroad.

Switching from the macro perspective to a micro analysis of the workings of the individual system, this study finds that the employees' handbook and workplace rules form the structure of governance in the workplace. The handbook resembles the collective bargaining agreement, but is not its equivalent. While most courts do not find that handbook promises are binding, challenges to its terms have led managements to include disclaimers to preserve their right to amend, modify, or cancel the handbook, and to deny any guarantee of continued employment. As for work rules, these exist in both union and nonunion workplaces, but management has an easier time in reshaping them under the individual than the organized system.

This study examined the question, is there a third way in employee relations in the United States? A group of academic specialists has recently argued that a model they call Nonunion Employee Representation, or NER, is an alternative to the organized system and to the individual system, although they neither acknowledge nor deny the existence of the individual system. This study rejects the claim that NER is an alternative either to the organized or the individual system because NERs are illegal in the United States. According to the definition of its proponents, NERs are set up by employers but nevertheless can negotiate terms of employment. Because they are involved in the governance of the workplace, under the National Labor Relations Act, NERs are illegal in this country. They exist in Canada by a quirk of history.

Another important and recent development in labor relations, employee participation plans, are also rejected by this study as an alternative to the organized or the individual system. Their principal function is to improve the efficiency of the company and avoid issues concerning the governance of the workplace. At this time, employee participation plans are in a legal no-man's land. Several have been declared in violation of the National Labor Relations Act as employer-dominated labor organizations and have been disestablished, but most continue to function because they do not deal with the governance of the workplace, as defined by the NLRB. If all forms of employee participation become legalized, they would add significant strength and efficiency to the individual system of representation.

This study argues that the labor market of the future will further boost the individual system. By the same token, and for other reasons, I also theorize that the organized system is headed into the *twilight zone in the next millennium.* By "twilight zone," I mean three things: First, a markedly reduced role for collective bargaining in the private economy of the United States and its restriction to a few key industries. Second, the private-sector organized system will probably enter the twenty-first century with almost the same market share it had at the beginning of the twentieth century. At that time it was 7 percent of private nonfarm employment, and at the turn of the new century, expect it to be about 9 percent. I have estimated that the unions would need 25 million new private-sector members, while holding on to all 9.3 million they now enroll, or a total membership of more than 35 million members, to regain their 1953 peak market share of 36 percent. To regain the peak membership population of 17 million of 1970 is also a hopeless task. To paraphrase a familiar political expression, "It's the numbers, stupid." The theory of the twilight zone also discounts the ability of new labor laws favorable to unions to enable them to stage a comeback. Again, based particularly on the experience of Canada, but also on the decline of private unionism among all other G-7 countries, I foresee no escape from the twilight zone.

In addition to the market forces that are steering the organized system into the twilight zone, unions have deep-seated internal problems, and these also presage no resurgence of the organized system in the new century. If it can be said that the success of unionization is a fairly direct function of the failure of management to discover and attend to employees' dissatisfaction, it can also be said that union leadership has failed to come to grips with the organized system's overriding problem: decline.

The long-run durability of the individual system depends on workers' demand for it and legal managerial policies to sustain it. Evidence from NLRB elections reported in Appendix Tables 1, 2, and 3 shows that the individual system is a successful and robust competitor in labor representation with every prospect for increasing its already enormous dominance. In my judgment, the continuing preeminence of the individual system is irrevocable.

The greatest potential challenge to the individual system in the new century, after a shift in workers' demand for the system, is management lapsing into hubris. Given the trends toward individual representation, managerial overconfidence could reap the harvest of unionism. Neglect of workers' problems has long been recognized by management as fertile ground for organizing. However, a major managerial relapse into neglect is unlikely. At the same time, I believe that most nonunion workers will continue to prefer a nonunion status in the future. Thus, the two conditions requisite for the system beyond unions and bargaining—workers' demand for individual representation, and employer preferences—will continue to hold into the future.

Appendix

Table 1

Total Votes for No Union in Unorganized Units, 1970–1997

	Total votes no union	Total votes all elections	No union percent
1970	211,632	502,489	42.1
1971	226,780	480,119	47.2
1972	207,683	489,332	42.4
1973	222,015	450,032	49.3
1974	230,936	449,758	51.3
1975	237,774	471,933	50.4
1976	201,260	383,601	52.5
1977	237,321	460,300	51.6
1978	197,565	376,483	52.5
1979	238,108	465,183	51.2
1980	217,684	415,048	52.4
1981	182,670	346,523	52.7
1982	113,879	210,487	54.1
1983	69,034	142,360	48.5
1984	84,020	170,941	49.2
1985	99,869	187,186	53.4
1986	123,112	229,573	53.6
1987	89,164	175,145	50.9
1988	93,749	183,237	51.2
1989	108,699	213,206	51.0
1990	106,258	201,238	52.8
1991	87,289	167,246	52.2
1992	85,835	161,221	53.2
1993	88,980	177,527	50.1
1994	86,019	164,044	52.4
1995	90,078	169,214	53.2
1996	87,554	190,338	46.0
1997	106.467	205,175	51.9
Averages	147,551	294,248	50.1

Source: National Labor Relations Board.

Table 2

Decertification Elections, 1970–1997

	Total	No union		Union win		Total votes No union[a]	Total Votes	Percent No union
		Number	%	Number	%			
1970	301	210	69.8	91	30.2	8,025	18,000	44.6
1971	401	279	69.6	122	30.4	9,110	18,062	50.4
1972	451	317	70.3	134	29.7	8,724	18,040	48.4
1973	453	315	69.5	138	30.5	7,902	17,112	46.2
1974	490	338	69.0	152	31.0	9,879	21,269	46.4
1975	516	379	73.4	137	26.6	11,304	20,110	56.2
1976	611	445	72.8	166	27.2	12,249	24,887	49.2
1977	849	645	76.0	204	24.0	18,761	35,769	52.5
1978	807	594	73.6	213	26.4	16,550	34,551	47.9
1979	777	583	75.0	194	25.0	17,320	33,474	51.7
1980	902	656	72.7	246	27.3	18,022	36,879	48.9
1981	856	641	74.9	215	25.1	21,286	39,254	54.2
1982	869	662	76.2	207	23.8	17,845	33,950	52.6
1983	922	690	74.8	232	25.2	18,665	33,425	55.8
1984	875	669	76.5	98	11.2	18,684	33,354	56.0
1985	865	654	75.6	211	24.4	18,708	31,724	59.0
1986	857	646	75.5	211	24.6	16,702	31,028	53.8
1987	755	575	76.2	180	23.8	18,013	32,721	55.1
1988	644	459	71.3	183	28.4	16,044	28,241	56.8
1989	622	441	70.9	181	29.1	12,270	22,703	54.0
1990	587	417	71.0	170	29.0	13,900	26,245	53.0
1991	573	400	69.8	173	30.2	13,961	26,340	53.0
1992	606	425	70.1	181	29.9	15,445	30,386	50.8
1993	531	366	68.9	165	31.1	11,961	21,548	55.5
1994	493	325	65.9	168	34.1	10,086	19,417	51.9
1995	488	345	70.7	143	29.3	9,975	18,786	53.1
1996	485	336	69.3	149	30.7	10,776	21,657	49.8
1997	405	278	68.6	127	31.4	8,503	16,167	52.6
Avg.	463	468	72.8	171	26.6	13,953	26,611	52.4

[a]Total nonunion votes in decertification elections is the sum of votes in elections unions won and lost.

Table 3

Representation Elections in Unorganized Units, 1970-1997

		No union win		Union win	
	Total	Number	%	Number	%
1970	7,426	3,212	43.3	4,214	56.7
1971	7,543	3,386	44.9	4,157	55.1
1972	8,066	3,583	44.4	4,483	55.6
1973	8,526	4,025	47.2	4,501	52.8
1974	7,994	3,863	48.3	4,131	51.7
1975	7,729	3,829	49.5	3,900	50.5
1976	7,736	3,830	49.5	3,906	50.5
1977	8,308	4,252	51.2	4,056	48.8
1978	7,168	3,664	51.1	3,504	48.9
1979	7,026	3,663	52.1	3,363	47.9
1980	7,021	3,580	51.0	3,441	49.0
1981	6,439	3,467	53.8	2,972	46.2
1982	4,031	2,223	55.1	1,808	44,9
1983	3,241	1,633	50.4	1,608	49.6
1984	3,336	1,738	52.1	1,598	47.9
1985	3,545	1,702	48.0	1,843	52.0
1986	3,479	1,827	52.5	1,652	47.5
1987	3,149	1,571	49.9	1,578	50.1
1988	3,377	1,700	50.3	1,677	49.7
1989	3,670	1,831	49.9	1,839	50.1
1990	3,536	1,763	49.9	1,773	50.1
1991	3,096	1,649	53.3	1,447	46.7
1992	2,924	1,475	50.4	1,449	49.6
1993	2,910	1,449	49.8	1,461	50.2
1994	3,020	1,539	51.0	1,481	49.0
1995	2,860	1,404	49.1	1,456	50.9
1996	2,738	1,436	52.4	1,302	47.6
1997	3,029	1,496	49.4	1,533	50.6
Avg.	5,104	2,538	49.5	2,576	50.5
Total	142,923	70,790	49.5	72,133	50.5

Source: National Labor Relations Board.

Figure 1. Nonunion Labor Market, 1900–2000

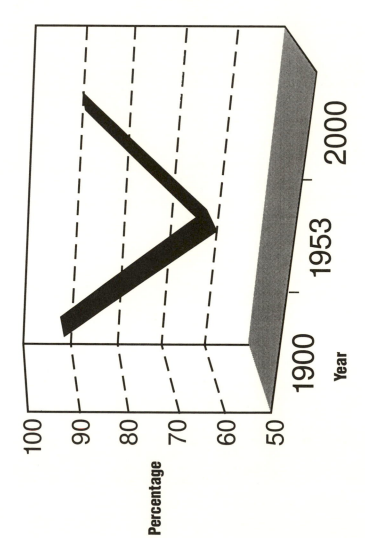

References

AFL-CIO Committee on the Evolution of Work. 1985. *The Changing Situation of Workers and Their Unions.* Washington, D.C.: American Federation of Labor and Congress of Industrial Organizations. February.

———. 1994. *The New American Workplace: A Labor Perspective.* Washington, D.C.: American Federation of Labor and Congress of Industrial Organizations. February.

Befort, Stephen F. 1991/1992. "Employee Handbooks and the Legal Effect of Disclaimers." *Relations Law Journal* 13, no. 2: 326–381.

Block, Richard N., and Jack Steiber. 1981. "U.S. Industrial Relations, 1950–1980: Summary and Conclusions." In *Industrial Relations, 1950–1980: A Critical Assessment,* ed. Jack Steiber, Robert B. McKersie, and Daniel Quinn Mills. Madison: Wisc.: University of Wisconsin. Industrial Relations Research Association Series.

Bluestone, Barry, and Bennet Harrison. 1982. *The Deindustrialization of America.* New York: Basic Books.

BLS. 1999. HTTP://www.bls.gov/news.release/union2.toc.htm.

Borgers, Frank, and Milan Lint. Circa 1993. "Industrial Relations in the Non-union Sector: Prospects and Problems." Manuscript, Ohio State University.

Brody, David. 1968. "The Rise and Fall of Welfare Capitalism." In *Change and Continuity in Twentieth Century America: The 1920s,* ed. John Braeman, Robert Bremmer, and David Brody, Columbus: Ohio State University Press.

Bronars, Stephen G., and Donald R. Deere. 1991. "The Threat of Unionization, the Use of Debt, and the Preservation of Shareholder Wealth." *Quarterly Journal of Economics* 106, no. 1 (February): 231–254.

———. 1989. "Union Organizing Activity and Union Coverage," 1973–1988. Manuscript. November.

———. 1988. "Union Organizing Activity and the Growth of Firms." Working Paper 26–89. University of California, Santa Barbara, Department of Economics. May.

Brown, Henry Phelps. 1990. "The Counter-Revolution of Our Time." *Industrial Relations* 29, no. 1: 1–14.

Bureau of National Affairs. 1996. *Daily Labor Report,* August 8.

———. 1997a. *Daily Labor Report.* February 13.

————. 1997b. *Daily Labor Report.* April 22.

————. 1999. *Daily Labor Report.* March 2.

Burgan, John U. 1985. "Cyclical Behavior of High Tech Industries." *Monthly Labor Review* 108, no. 5 (May): 9–15.

Burns, Arthur F. 1934. *Production Trends in the U.S. Since 1870.* New York: National Bureau of Economic Research.

Canadian Federation of Labour. 1990. *Assessment of General Public and Membership: Attitudes toward Labour Unions, the Canadian Federation of Labour and Related Issues.* Toronto: Canadian Federation of Labour. June.

Capelli, Peter, and John Chalykoff. 1975. "The Effects of Management Industrial Relations Strategy: Results of a Recent Survey." *38th Annual Proceedings.* Industrial Relations Research Association.

Cimini, Michael, Susan L. Berman, and Eric M. Johnson, 1993. "Labor-Management Bargaining in 1992." *Monthly Labor Review* 116, no. 1 (January): 19–34.

Claydon, Tim. 1989. "Union Derecognition in Britain in the 1980s." *British Journal of Industrial Relations* 27, no. 2 (July): 214–224.

Delery, John F. 1997. "Human Resource Management in the USA." In *The Blackwell Encyclopedic Dictionary of Human Resource Management,* ed. Lawrence H. Peters, Charles R. Greer, and Susan A. Youngblood. Oxford: Blackwell Business, pp. 150–53.

Derber, Milton. 1982. "Are We in a New Stage?" Presidential address. Proceedings of the Thirty-Fifth Annual Meeting, Industrial Relations Research Association. December 28–30, pp. 1–9.

Dubofsky, Melvyn. 1986. "Industrial Relations: Comparing the 1920s with the 1980s." Proceedings of the Industrial Relations Research Association. Madison, Wisc.: pp. 227–236.

Duncan, Greg J., and Frank P. Stafford. 1980. "Do Union Members Receive Compensating Wage Differentials?" *American Economic Review* 70, no. 3 (June): 355–371.

Dunlop, John T. 1958. *Industrial Relations Systems.* New York: Henry Holt.

————. 1978. "Past and Future Tendencies in American Labor Organizations." *Daedalus* 107, no. 1 (Winter): 79–98.

Electromation, Inc. 309 NLRB 990 (1992). Enforced, 35 F. 3d 1148 (7th Cir. 1994); E.I. Dupont de Nemours & Co., 311 NLRB 893 (1993).

Epstein, Richard A. 1975. "Grievance Procedure in Non-Union Setting—Caveat Employer. *Employment Relations Law Journal* 1, no. 1: 120–127.

————. 1992. "As Unions Decline, Labor Laws Constrain the Job Market." *Wall Street Journal,* September 2, p. A11.

Estreicher, Samuel. 1998. "Nonunion Employee Representation: A Legal/Policy Perspective." Manuscript.

Ewing, David W. 1977. *Freedom inside the Organization: Bringing Civil Liberties to the Workplace.* New York: Dutton.

————. 1989. *Justice on the Job: Resolving Grievances in the Nonunion Workplace.* Boston: Harvard Business School Press.

Fabricant, Solomon. 1942. *Employment in Manufacturing, 1899–1939.* New York: National Bureau of Economic Research.

Working paper 2877. Cambridge, Mass.: National Bureau of Economic Research. February.

Farber, Henry S., and Alan B. Kreuger. 1992. "Union Membership in the United States: The Decline Continues." Working paper 4216. Cambridge, Mass.: National Bureau of Economics Research. November. This paper also appears in Bruce E. Kaufman, and Morris M. Kleiner, eds., *Employee Representation: Alternatives and Future Directions.* Madison, Wisc.: Industrial Relations Research Association, 1993.

Foulkes, Fred. 1980. *Personnel Policies in Large Nonunion Companies.* Englewood Cliffs, N.J.: Prentice Hall.

Franklin, James C. 1997. "Industry Output and Employment Projections to 2006." *Monthly Labor Review* 120, no. 11 (November): 39–57.

Freedman, Audrey. 1982. "A Fundamental Change in Wage Bargaining." *Challenge* 25, no. 3 (July-August): 14–17.

Freeman, Richard B. 1986. "Unionism Comes to the Public Sector." *Journal of Economic Literature* 24, no. 1 (March): 41–86.

———. 1994. "Worker Representation and Participation Survey: Second Report of Findings." Appendix. In the *Final Report of the Commission on the Future of Work.* December.

Freeman, Richard B., and Morris M. Kleiner. 1990. "Employer Behavior in the Face of Union Organizing Drives." *Industrial and Labor Relations Review* 43, no. 4 (April): 351–355.

Freeman, Richard B., and James Medoff. 1984. *What Do Unions Do?* New York: Basic Books.

Freeman, Richard B., and Joel Rogers. 1993. "Who Speaks for Us? Employee Representation in a Nonunion Labor Market." In *Employee Representation: Alternatives and Future Directions,* ed. Bruce E. Kaufman, and Morris M. Kleiner. Madison, Wisc.: Industrial Relations Association Research Series.

———. 1997. "What Do Workers Want? Voice, Representation, and Power in the American Workplace." Paper read at the 50th New York University Annual Conference on Labor, New York, May.

Friedman, Milton. 1980. *Free to Choose: A Personal Statement.* New York: Harcourt.

Friedman, Sheldon, and Lydia Fischer. 1988. "Collective Bargaining and Employment Security." Paper read at the 41st Meeting of the Industrial Relations Research Association. December.

Fuchs, Victor. 1968. *The Service Economy.* New York: National Bureau of Economic Research.

Garbarino, Joseph W. 1984. "Unionism Without Unions: The New Industrial Relations?" *Industrial Relations* 23, no. 1 (Winter): 40–51.

Goldfield, Michael. 1982. "The Decline of Organized Labor: NLRB Union Certification Election Results." *Politics and Society* 11, no. 2:167–209.

Greenhouse, Steven. 1999. "In Biggest Drive Since 1937, Union Gains a Victory." *New York Times,* February 26, p. A1:3.

Hamermesh, Daniel. 1988. "Shirking and Productive Schmoozing: Wages and the Allocation of Time at Work." Working paper 2800. Cambridge, Mass: National Bureau of Economic Research. December.

Harris, Louis, and Associates. 1984. *A Study on the Outlook for Trade Union Organizing*. Study 843008. November.

Heywood, John S. 1989. "Do Union Members Receive Compensating Differentials? The Case of Employment Security." *Journal of Labor Research* 10, no. 3 (Summer): 271–283.

Hills, Stephen M. 1985. "The Attitudes of Union and Nonunion Male Workers Toward Union Representation," *Industrial and Labor Relations Review* 38, no. 2: 179–194.

Hirsch, Barry T. 1991. *Labor Unions and the Economic Performance of Firms*. Kalamazoo, Mich.: W.E. Upjohn Institute for Employment Research.

———. 1997. "Unionization and Economic Performance." In *Unions and Right-to-Work Law,* ed. Fazil Mihlar. Vancouver, Canada: Fraser Institute, pp. 35–70.

Hirsch, Barry T., and David A. Macpherson. 1998. *Union Membership and Earnings Data Book*. Washington, D.C.: Bureau of National Affairs.

Imai, Hitoshi. 1998. "The Making of the Modern Labor Management in the Ford Motor Company." In *How Nonunion Industrial Relations Systems Work: Corporate Labor Policies and the Workers in the U.S., 1920s,* ed. Hirao Takehisa, Akira Morikawa, Kenichi Ito, and Teiichi Sekiguchi. Hokkaido, Japan: Hokkaido University Press.

Irving, John S. 1994. "Employee Participation Committees." Paper read before the Labor and Employment Law Symposium, Los Angeles County Bar Association, March 4.

Jacoby, Sanford M. 1986. "Labor's Changing Agenda: How the Eighties Parallel the Twenties." *Management* (University of California–Los Angeles) 6, no. 1 (Fall): 13–14, 20.

Kaufman, Bruce. 1997. "The Future of the Labor Movement." *Labor Law Journal* 48, no. 4 (August): 474–484.

Kaufman, Bruch, and Daphne Gottlieb Taras. 1999. *Nonunion Employee Representation*. Armonk, N.Y.: M.E. Sharpe.

Keddy, John. 1988. "Econometric Analysis of American Trade Union Growth: New Evidence." Honors paper, Rutgers University, New Jersey. April. Mimeographed.

Keller, Harry. 1990. *Why Unions Are in Trouble . . . and What They Can Do about It*. New York: Trade Union Leadership Institute.

Kerr, Clark, John T. Dunlop, Frederick H. Harbison, and Charles A. Myers. 1960. *Industrialism and Industrial Man: The Problems of Labor and Management in Economic Growth*. Cambridge: Harvard University Press; 2nd edition, New York: Oxford University Press, 1964.

Kochan, Thomas A. 1995. "Using the Dunlop Report to Full Advantage: A Strategy for Achieving Mutual Gains." Catherwood Library, Cornell University. January. (http://www.ilr.cornell.edu/library/e_archive/Dunlop/Kochan.html)

Kochan, Thomas A., Harry C. Katz, and Robert B. McKersie. 1986. *The Transformation of American Industrial Relations*. New York: Basic Books.

LaLonde, Robert J., Bernard D. Meltzer. 1991. "Hard Times for Unions: Another Look at the Significance of Employer Illegalities." *University of Chicago Law Review* 58, no. 3 (Summer): 953–1014.

LaLonde, Robert J., Gerard Marschke, and Kenneth Troske. 1996. "Using Longitudinal Data on Establishments to Analyze the Effects of Union Organizing Campaigns in the United States." *Annales D'Economie Et De Statistique* 41/42 (January–June): 155–185.

Leibowitz, Ann G. 1997. "The 'Non-union Union?'" Paper read at the 50th New York University Annual Conference on Labor, New York, May.

LeRoy, Michael H. 1997. "Employee Involvement Programs and §8(a)(2): A Survey of Employer Practices." Paper read at the 50th New York University Annual Conference on Labor, New York, May.

Levin, Doron. 1989. "Nissan Workers in the U.S. Test Union and Industry." *New York Times,* August 12.

Lewin, David. 1990. "Symposium on Labor Arbitration Thirty Years After the Steelworkers Trilogy: Grievance Procedures in Nonunion Workplaces: An Empirical Analysis of Usage, Dynamics, and Outcomes." *Chicago-Kent Law Review* 66: 823–844.

Lewin, David, Daniel J.B. Mitchell, and Mahmood Zaidi. 1997. "Separating Ideas and Bubbles in Human Resource Management." In *The Human Resource Management Handbook.* Part I. David Lewin, Daniel J.B. Mitchell, and Mahmood Zaidi. Greenwich, Conn.: JAI Press.

Lewis, H. Greg. 1986. *Union Relative Wage Effects.* Chicago: University of Chicago Press.

Lindbloom, Charles E. 1949. *Unions and Capitalism.* New Haven: Yale University Press.

Lipset, S. Martin, and Noah Meltz. 1996. "Comparative Labour Attitudes Survey. Preliminary Survey Data." Manuscript. September 13.

Little, Jane Sneedon. 1989. "Exchange Rates and Structural Change in U.S. Manufacturing Employment." *New England Economic Review,* March/April, pp. 56–70.

Long, Richard J. 1993. "The Effects of Unionization on Employment Growth of Canadian Companies." *Industrial and Labor Relations Review* 46, no. 4 (July): 691–703.

———. 1997. "Motives for Profit Sharing: A Study of Canadian Chief Executive Officers." *Industrial Relations-Relations Industrielles* 52, no. 4 (Fall): 712–733.

Machan, Tibor R. 1981. "Some Philosophical Aspects of National Labor Policy." *Harvard Journal of Law and Public Policy* 4 (Summer): 67–160.

McCabe, Douglas M. 1988. *Corporate Nonunion Complaint Procedures and Systems.* New York: Praeger.

McLoughlin, Ian P., and Ian J. Beardwell. 1989. "Nonunionism and the Non-Union Firm in British Industrial Relations." Occasional paper 7. Kingston Polytechnic, School of Industrial Relations and Personnel Management, Kingston, England. January.

McMahan, Gary C., and Lawler, Edward E. III. 1994. *Effects Of Union Status On Employee Involvement: Diffusion and Effectiveness.* Washington, DC: Employment Policy Foundation.

Masters, Marick F., and Robert S. Atkin. 1997. "The Finances of Major U.S. Unions." *Industrial Relations* 30, no. 4 (October): 489–506.

Medoff, James L. 1977. "The Public Image of Labor and Labor's Response." Manuscript. December.

Mills, Daniel Quinn. 1986. *Labor-Management Relations.* New York: McGraw-Hill.

Myers, M. Scott. 1976. *Managing Without Unions.* Reading, Mass.: Addison-Wesley.

Nelson, David. 1982. "The Company Union Movement, 1900–1937: A Reexamination." *Business History Review* 56, no. 3 (Autumn): 335–357.

Neumann, George, and Ellen R. Rissman. 1984. "Where Have All the Union Members Gone?" *Journal of Labor Economics* 2, no. 2 (April): 175–192.

Noble, Kenneth B. 1988. "Harvard's Chief Battles Union Drive." *New York Times,* May 16, p. A12: 1.

Ozanne, Robert. 1967. *A Century of Labor-Management Relations at McCormick and International Harvester.* Madison: University of Wisconsin Press.

Patterson, Gregory A. 1989. "Disunited Labor." *Wall Street Journal.*

Penn, Mark, and Douglas Schoen. 1993. *National Poll Shows Public Wants from Labor Law Commission.* Press Release. Employment Policy Foundation. Washington: D.C.

Perl, Peter. 1987. "The Life-Line for Unions: Recruiting." *Washington Post,* September 13, p. H 1.

Perlman, Mark. 1968. "Labor in Eclipse." In *Change and Continuity in the Twentieth Century: The 1920s,* ed. John Braeman, Robert Bremmer, and David Brody. Columbus: Ohio State University Press.

Potter, Edward E. 1991. *Quality at Risk: Are Employee Participation Programs in Jeopardy?* Washington, D.C.: Employment Policy Foundation.

Public Broadcasting System. 1995. "The State of the Unions," *Think Tank,* November 3. (http://www.pbs.org/thinktank/archive/transcripts/transcript.232.html)

Raff, Daniel, and Lawrence H. Summers. 1987. "Did Henry Ford Pay Efficiency Wages?" *Journal of Labor Economics* 5, no. 4 (October): Part 2 S 57–86.

Ruben, George S. 1987. "Labor-Management Scene in 1986 Reflects Continuing Difficulties." *Monthly Labor Review* 110, no. 1 (January): 37–48.

Samuelson, Paul A., and William D. Nordhaus. 1985. *Economics.* 12th ed. New York: McGraw-Hill.

Sheflin, Neil. 1984. "Transition Function Estimation of Structural Shifts in Models of American Trade Union Growth." *Applied Economics* 16, no. 1: 73–80.

Sheflin, Neil, Leo Troy, and Timothy Koeller. 1981. "Structural Stability in Models of Trade Union Growth." *Quarterly Journal of Economics* 96, no. 1 (February): 77–88.

Silvestri, George T. 1997. "Occupational Employment Projections to 2006." *Monthly Labor Review* 120, no. 11 (November): 58–83.

Slichter, Sumner. 1948. *Trade Unions in a Free Society.* Cambridge: Harvard University Press.

St. Antoine, Theodore J. 1988. "A Seed Germinates: Unjust Discharge Reform Heads Toward Full Flower." *Nebraska Law Review* 67, no. 1 and 2: 56–81.

Stone, Thomas H., and Noah M. Meltz. 1993. *Human Resource Management in Canada.* 3rd ed. Toronto: Holt, Rinehart and Winston, 1993.

Taras, Daphne G. 1997. "Why Nonunion Representation Is Legal in Canada." *Industrial Relations-Relations Industrielles* 52, no. 4 (Fall): 763–786.

Taras, Daphne G., and Jason Copping. 1998. "The Transition from Formal Nonunion Representation to Unionization: A Contemporary Case." *Industrial and Labor Relations Review* 52, no. 1 (October): 22–44.

Troy, Leo. 1960. "Local Independent and National Unions: Competitive Labor Organizations." *Journal of Political Economy* 68, no. 5 (October): 487–506.

———. 1990."Will a More Interventionist NLRA Revive Organized Labor?" *Harvard Journal of Law and Public Policy* 13, no. 2 (Spring): 583–634.

———. 1997. "The Twilight of the Old Unionism." In *The Human Resource Management Handbook,* David Lewin; Daniel J.B. Mitchell; and Mahmood Zaidi, eds. Greenwich, Conn.: JAI Press.

———. 1999. "U.S. and Canadian Industrial Relations, Convergent or Divergent?" Manuscript.

Troy, Leo, and Neil Sheflin. 1985. *Union Sourcebook.* West Orange, N.J.: Industrial Relations Data and Information Services.

U.S. Small Business Administration, Office of Advocacy. 1998. *Economic Statistics and Research on Small Business.* (http://www.sba.gov/ADVO/stats/)

U.S. Department of Labor and U.S. Department of Commerce. Commission on the Future of Worker-Management Relations. 1994a. *Fact Finding Report.* Washington, D.C.: The Commission, May.

———. 1994b. *Report and Recommendations.* Washington, D.C.: The Commission, December.

Verma, Anil. 1983. "Union and Nonunion Industrial Relations Systems at the Plant Level." Ph. D. dissertation, Massachusetts Institute of Technology.

Voos, Paula B., and Lawrence R. Mishel. 1986. "The Union Impact on Profits: Evidence from Industry Price-Cost Margin Data." *Journal of Labor Economics* 4, no. 1: 105–133.

Webb, Sidney, and Beatrice Webb. 1920. *Industrial Democracy.* London, New York, Bombay, Calcutta, and Madras:Longmans, Green and Co..

Weiler, Paul. 1983. "Promises to Keep: Securing Workers' Rights to Self-Organization under the NLRA." *Harvard Law Review* 96, no. 8 (June): 1769–1827.

———. 1988. "The Representation Gap in the American Workplace." Paper read before the American Bar Association Annual Meeting, Toronto, Canada, August.

———. 1990. *Governing the Work Place: The Future of Labor and Employment Law.* Cambridge: Harvard University Press.

Wever, Kirsten. 1995. *Negotiating Competitiveness.* Boston: Harvard Business School Press.

Index

About the Author

Leo Troy is Professor of Economics, Rutgers University–Newark. He has taught at Rutgers for more than forty years. Professor Troy earned his Ph.D. in economics from Columbia University; he is a member of Phi Beta Kappa. He has received numerous awards for his scholarship, including two from the National Science Foundation, and two Fulbright Visiting Professorships to England. He has published widely in the field of labor over the last half-century and has been published in leading journals in this country and in the United Kingdom. Among these journals are the *Harvard Journal of Law and Public Policy*, The *University of Chicago Law Review*, the *British Journal of Industrial Relations*, *Industrial Relations* (Berkeley), the *Industrial and Labor Relations Review*, the *Journal of Labor Research*, and *Advances in Industrial Relations Research*. He has contributed chapters to several books including, most recently, one on the teachers' unions. His most recent book was *The New Unionism and the New Society*. Professor Troy worked for many years at the National Bureau of Economic Research, a nonprofit organization in New York City, which published a number of his works. Professor Troy is also the author of the *Almanac of Business and Industrial Financial Ratios*, published by Prentice Hall for the past thirty years. The *Almanac* is distributed worldwide.

His scholarship is widely recognized outside academia. He has been cited in some 200 newspaper, magazine, and wire accounts over the past few years. These include the *Wall Street Journal*, the *New York Times*, the *Los Angeles Times*, the *Washington Post*, USA

Today, the *Journal of Commerce*, *Roll Call*, and regional papers across the country, as well as numerous wire services. Outside the United States, he has been interviewed and cited by the *Toronto Globe and Mail* and in French newspapers. He has been interviewed and cited by leading business magazines, such as *Fortune* and *Forbes*, and has been interviewed frequently on radio, including National Public Radio, the BBC World Service, and French National Radio. He has also lectured abroad for the U.S. Information Agency.

Professor Troy is a veteran of World War II with three battle stars and the combat infantry badge. He is the father of two children and the grandfather of three children, two of whom are twins.